Throne for Two

The Secret Marital Battles of Kings and Queens, From Palace Intrigues to Divorce Courts: How Royal Couples Really Live When the Cameras Stop Rolling

Nicole Levington
&
Ted Shubbard

Throne for Two

The Secret Marital Battles of Kings and Queens, From Palace
Intrigues to Divorce Courts: How Royal Couples Really Live
When the Cameras Stop Rolling

CROSSBORDER

New York, London, Quebec

Contents

Introduction

Fairy tales end with "happily ever after," but real royal marriages? They end with prenups, separate bedrooms, and the occasional beheading. Behind the gilded gates and ceremonial pageantry lies a truth more scandalous than any tabloid headline: crowned heads make terrible spouses.

Consider the paradox of absolute power meeting marital compromise. When you can command armies but can't get your husband to put down the toilet seat, tensions arise. When your wife controls the royal treasury but you control the royal guard, dinner conversations become delicate diplomatic negotiations.

From Henry VIII's creative approach to divorce proceedings to modern monarchs navigating paparazzi and marriage counselors, royal couples have always faced a unique challenge: maintaining domestic bliss while running nations, dodging assassins, and looking photogenic during state dinners.

These pages chronicle the magnificent disasters, petty squabbles, and occasionally genuine romance that unfold when unlimited power meets limited patience. Discover how royal marriages survive (or spectacularly don't) when the stakes include both personal happiness and international incidents.

Welcome to the ultimate reality show: where crowns clash, kingdoms hang in the balance, and someone always sleeps in the guest palace.

Ted and I (Nicole) thank you advance for choosing our book. We promise you will enjoy it.

Chapter 1

The Gilded Fairy Tale (Myth vs. Reality)

Fairy-Tale Facades

Royal weddings always look like something out of a storybook – glittering crowns, horse-drawn carriages, adoring crowds, and a kiss on the balcony for the cameras. It's the ultimate happily-ever-after image, right? But step beyond those palace gates and you'll find that the magic often fades into the mundane once the honeymoon is over. The reality of royal matrimony isn't all tiaras and tea parties; sometimes it's more like trying to waltz in steel-toed boots. Fairy tales promise that princes and princesses ride off into the sunset, but actual palace life can feel more like they're stuck in rush-hour traffic on the way to couples' counseling.

Every time a royal pair ties the knot, the world swoons over the "fairy-tale" romance. We eat up those perfect public images – the beaming bride in a designer gown, the dashing groom in full military regalia (with medals he might not even remember earning), and the two of them waving from a gilded carriage as if all their problems have magically vanished. It's a beautiful facade, and we love to believe in it. We want to think that kings and queens live an enchanted life where arguments are as rare as dragon sightings. After all, isn't that why we call it a fairy tale? The phrase "happily ever after" had to come from somewhere, and a palace seems as good a place as any to find it.

Yet behind that shining facade, history and gossip remind us that royal marriages can be just as snakebitten as anyone else's. Even centuries ago people understood that marriage is a gamble, no matter who you are. Royal status doesn't change that fact – kings and queens were never immune to the lucky dip of matrimony. Thomas More's father famously warned that getting married is like reaching into a sack full of snakes and only a few eels: odds are you're going to pull out a snake instead of an eel. In other words, you never quite know what you're going to get. This bit of reptilian wisdom applies even if you're a monarch. A king may snag a princess for a bride, but he might still end up feeling like he grabbed a viper by mistake (and some queens have felt the same way about their charming princes!). When reality sets in, the "perfect" royal couple might discover that uneasy lies the head that wears the crown – and even uneasier lies the head sharing the royal pillow.

Take for example the famously fairy-tale wedding of Prince Charming and his lovely princess in our collective imagination – or better yet, a real historical couple like Prince Charles and Lady Diana. Their 1981 wedding was literally billed as a "fairy tale come to life," watched by hundreds of millions around the globe. She was young, beautiful, and shy; he was the dashing heir to the throne. They rode in that golden coach and waved like actors in a Disney movie.

But behind the scenes? Let's just say the script didn't have a happily ever after. The magic carriage turned back into a pumpkin in record time.

Publicly they smiled and danced at balls, but privately their marriage stumbled under the weight of mutual unhappiness, misunderstandings, and a third person who didn't fit the fairy-tale narrative. *Spoiler alert:* real life refused to stay politely offstage.

The truth is that being royal doesn't grant you a free pass from the normal irritations of married life. Sure, you might not be arguing about whose turn it is to take out the trash – palace staff probably has that chore covered (lucky them) – but you'll find something else to bicker about. Maybe it's the Queen's habit of letting her corgis on the antique furniture, or the King leaving wet towels on an 18th-century velvet chair. Perhaps the grand ball was scheduled on the same night as your anniversary (how rude!), or one of you gave a priceless heirloom tiara to the wrong cousin by accident. These aren't the kinds of problems we commoners face, but they can cause just as much eye-rolling and exasperated sighing in a palace as a clogged sink might in a suburban home.

The gilded fairy tale that we see from the outside is just that – a shiny story, a well-edited movie trailer for a much messier film. Royal couples have to keep up the image of perfection, but once they're in the privacy of their chambers, the reality hits. You can almost imagine a weary queen kicking off her satin heels, rubbing her sore feet, and grumbling, "Happily ever after? Sure – right after I finish dealing with this royal mess in the kitchen." The fairy-tale facade is fun for the public, but inside the castle walls, it's often a different story entirely.

The Crown's Weight at Home

Being the sovereign of a nation is a full-time job that doesn't end when the crown comes off at night. All those pressures of ruling a country have a way of crashing right through the palace doors and into the royal bedroom. Imagine trying to balance state duties with date nights: one minute you're planning a quiet dinner with your spouse, the next minute an aide bursts in announcing a crisis in the kingdom that simply can't wait. Cue the royal eye roll.

In a normal family, you might have to reschedule a movie night because one of the kids is sick; in a royal family, you reschedule because the Prime Minister needs an urgent chat or there's an ambassador waiting in the hallway. Duty calls at the most inconvenient times, and it doesn't care if it's your anniversary or if you were just about to finally discuss that thing your partner said last week that's been bothering you.

The result can be unintentionally comic. Picture a monarch literally penciling in a lovers' quarrel for later: "Darling, I know you're furious with me, but could we postpone this argument until after the state dinner? I have to go toast the visiting dignitaries in five minutes." It sounds absurd, but it happens. Royal couples often find themselves squeezing their personal disagreements into the few free slivers of time on the schedule. Nothing says marital bliss like scheduling your spat around a ribbon-cutting ceremony. They might dress in finery and appear composed in front of the cameras, but behind closed doors they're watching the clock, waiting for the moment they can pick up their tiff where they left off (hopefully after the guests have gone home).

Even when they do get to spend time together, the crown's influence is never far away. Who gets to hold the remote control for the TV in a palace? You might joke that the King's word is law, but try telling that to a Queen who's midway through her favorite show. The battle for the remote can become the battle of the remote scepter – because everything sounds grander when you're royal, even channel surfing. Sure, it's a trivial domestic squabble, but layer on the fact that one of you technically rules an entire nation and suddenly the power dynamics get weird. Does the reigning monarch automatically get to pick what to watch on Netflix (or the royal equivalent)? Or is home the one place where the crown gets hung on the coat rack and it's an equal playing field? These are questions no fairy tale ever addresses, but real royals have to figure out.

In fact, the very hierarchy that defines a monarchy can tip the scales in a marriage. When the King or Queen is used to everyone standing when they enter a room and never being contradicted, how do they handle a spouse who might, for example, point out that they've left their socks on the floor again or that their brilliant idea to redecorate the palace in purple isn't actually so brilliant? It's a recipe for domestic drama. The Queen might outrank her prince consort in public ceremonies, but at home he may want to feel like "the man of the house" – cue a clash of wills worthy of a Shakespeare play (but playing out over the breakfast table). A historical example: Britain's Prince Philip reportedly bristled at having to live in Queen Elizabeth II's royal shadow early on. He couldn't even give his last name to their children without a constitutional fuss – imagine the dinner-table tension of *that* discussion. ("Oh, so my name isn't good enough for our own kids, Liz? Is that what you're saying?")

The crown's weight isn't just heavy on the monarch's head; it puts pressure on their marriage, too.

At the end of the day, high status doesn't automatically translate to a happy home. There's a constant juggle between public duty and private life. One mistimed royal duty – say, a king spending an extra hour schmoozing foreign envoys – can leave his queen feeling like he cares more about the kingdom than about her. Conversely, a queen preoccupied with her charitable foundation might miss her husband's big polo match, leaving him feeling underappreciated. These are the kind of royal growing pains that don't make it into the news headlines, but they're very real. Uneasy lies the head that wears the crown, indeed – and uneasy sits the spouse beside that head, waiting for their turn to have a normal conversation that isn't interrupted by a royal advisor clearing his throat in the doorway.

Public Smiles, Private Strife

If you've ever seen a royal couple at a public event, they look flawless – all radiant smiles, gracious waves, and maybe even coordinated outfits in just the right shades of pastel. The message is clear: together, they are picture-perfect. But behind those smiling selfies and polished appearances, there may be a very different conversation happening once the cameras are off. Royals have mastered the art of the poker-face photocall. They can be seething inwardly about something as mundane as a misplaced shoe or as serious as a brewing scandal, yet still project unity and charm in front of the public. It's practically a job requirement: never let the mask slip, at least not where the press might see.

The contrast between public and private is often stark. In public, a king and queen might hold hands for the first time in months just because they're dedicating a new hospital wing and the world's media is watching. They'll gaze into each other's eyes for the camera as if they share every thought and have never once disagreed about anything more contentious than what tea to have for breakfast. Meanwhile, in private, they could be locked in a passive-aggressive battle over who left the cap off the royal toothpaste.

Perhaps they were debating the night before about whether their eldest should attend a regular school for a "normal" childhood or be tutored behind palace walls. Maybe they're mid-debate on something truly earth-shattering like which shade of gold to paint the new nursery. (He wants traditional gilded baroque, she wants a more modern subtle champagne hue – oh, the drama!) Whatever the issue, they've likely developed a skill set any undercover spy would envy: smiling through it and acting like all is well, even if a storm is brewing at home.

One day they're literally on the cover of every magazine, hailed as the perfect couple, and later that evening they might be giving each other the cold shoulder across a ridiculously long dining table because of some argument nobody would believe royals actually have. Think about it – we've all had to put on a polite face in front of guests right after squabbling with our partner. Royal couples just have to do that in front of an entire nation (and a phalanx of paparazzi). No pressure or anything! It could be that during that graceful balcony wave, the queen is still fuming that the king forgot their anniversary, or the king is grinding his teeth because the queen teased him about his speech slip-up. But you'd never know it from the smiles pasted on their faces. Public events are their stage, and they are consummate actors on it.

Insiders have whispered over the years about what really goes on behind palace doors. Servants and aides see a lot – the tense silences, the icy stares, maybe even the occasional vase or shoe being hurled in frustration. (In fact, one famous tale from the 1950s had Queen Elizabeth II chucking a shoe and a tennis racket at Prince Philip during a heated quarrel on a royal tour. Minutes later, they stepped outside their tent all smiles and waves, as if the only flying object had been a harmless butterfly.) These kinds of stories usually stay hush-hush until decades later, when some biographer or loose-lipped butler spills the beans, confirming what we suspected all along: the royals are human, and marriage can be tricky even when you're wearing a crown.

For the public image, though, it's all about unity and decorum. A royal couple's life is a bit like an Instagram feed versus reality: the photos show immaculate outfits, cute family moments, and fairytale romance, while the reality might involve disagreements about how to discipline the kids or whose turn it is to visit the in-laws this weekend (imagine scheduling that around a public appearance!). Palace PR teams work overtime to maintain the illusion of the flawless royal family. They issue those glowing press releases and stage those perfect family portraits, cropping out any evidence of discord (both literal and metaphorical). And to their credit, many royal couples do genuinely care for each other – they just also happen to drive each other crazy sometimes, like any long-married pair. The difference is, when your job is being a symbol of national stability, you learn to bury the strife under a thick layer of protocol and polite smiles until you're back in privacy where the crowns come off and the gloves (maybe literally) come off too.

Royals: They're (Almost) Just Like Us

Strip away the ermine robes and the fancy titles, and a royal marriage starts to look surprisingly like any other marriage – just with a lot more staff involved and a much bigger house. At their core, these are two people trying to make a life together, and they deal with many of the same issues the rest of us do. Sure, their anniversary gifts might be on a different scale (when a queen says she wants *a little something special*, her king might present her with a small country or at least a duchy, whereas the rest of us are maxing out the credit card on a nice dinner and maybe a new coffee maker). But the thought and the potential for disappointment are universal – even a queen can roll her eyes if her royal hubby truly thought a jewel-encrusted ostrich feather was an appropriate birthday gift. It's the effort that counts, right?

In-laws? Oh, they have those too, in spades. And you better believe there's drama. If you think your mother-in-law has opinions, imagine the dowager queen or the king's mother weighing in on everything from how the royal children are raised to how the palace should be run. A modern princess might get subtle shade from the Queen Mother about her fashion choices or how she's doing her royal duties ("In *my* day, dear, we curtseyed lower and never spoke about our feelings in public"). Historically, some kings' mothers or queens' fathers acted like they were still in charge, turning family dinners into a stealth continuation of court politics. Sound familiar? Many couples deal with parental interference – it's just that when royals do it, the whole kingdom might feel the ripples.

Mid-life crises? Check. The stereotypical middle-aged guy might splurge on a sports car; a bored king in a mid-life funk could commission a new royal yacht or start a quixotic war in an exotic land (anything to feel alive again!). A queen feeling restless might decide to take up a bizarre hobby or adopt a hundred new charitable patronages overnight. It might not be the red convertible and new haircut that a commoner opts for, but the sentiment is the same: "I need something new in my life!" Royal or not, people get the itch for change, and their spouses have to buckle up for the ride. One day the king is brooding over the meaning of life; the next he's insisting on a grand refurbishing of the palace stables because *that's* his new passion. The queen just smiles and lets him have at it – much like any wife humoring her husband's sudden obsession with woodworking in the garage, except substitute *garage* with, you know, an entire wing of the palace.

And of course, the classic marital spats don't spare the blue-bloods. Even with a retinue of servants, a prince can forget to put the toilet seat down (yes, even a gold-plated toilet still has a seat that goes up and down). A queen might hog the bathroom counter with her assortment of potions and perfumes, leaving the king's side a royal mess. He might snore loud enough to rattle the palace windows, driving her to exile him to a distant chamber for the night. She might have a habit of talking through his favorite part of the opera. He might secretly hate the cook's signature venison stew that she loves. These little irritations are the stuff of everyday marriage. The difference is, when royals bicker about someone leaving dirty boots in the hallway, there's probably a footman standing by pretending to be a statue, politely ignoring Their Majesties' tiff while internally thinking, "Here we go again."

At the heart of it, a royal marriage requires compromise and communication just like any other. Maybe even more so, given the high stakes and high stress. They have to juggle love and duty, personal desires and public expectations. That means learning to meet in the middle: perhaps she agrees to let him have his weekly hunting trip with the guys as long as he attends the ballet with her next time; he concedes to naming their daughter after her side of the family if she lets him off the hook for a few state banquets. They figure it out, through gritted teeth or genuine laughter, because that's what couples do. Royal status doesn't magically bestow relationship bliss – it just adds more layers (and more people watching).

So yes, royals really are almost just like us when it comes to marriage. They argue, they make up, they laugh at private jokes, they endure each other's quirks. The king might give a grand speech about national unity in the morning, then come home and unite with his queen in exasperation over their teenagers' terrible taste in music. The queen might spend the afternoon opening a children's hospital with grace and charm, then that night collapse on the couch next to her husband in sweatpants (fine, a cashmere tracksuit) to binge-watch a favorite show. It's a life of contrasts. This irreverent peek behind the velvet curtain reminds us that even in palaces and castles, marriage means partnership and patience – just with more gilding on the surface and perhaps a courtier or two in the wings to witness the occasional royal eye-roll.

In the end, a throne is just a fancy chair, and marriage is still marriage – with or without a crown. Royals or not, it's two people figuring out life together (just with a bit more gold leaf on the furniture).

Chapter 2

Arranged and Deranged – Duty, Dynasty, and "I Do"

Royal marriage has rarely been the fairy tale of soulmates locking eyes across a crowded throne room. More often, it was the medieval equivalent of a corporate merger sealed with a kiss (or at least a stiff bow). In centuries past, when kings and queens said "I do," what they really meant was "I oblige" – not to each other, but to country and crown. Romance took a backseat (perhaps in a far carriage behind the royal coach) while duty drove the pair down the aisle. The result? Monarchs were often married to the throne, not each other, and their hapless hearts served as bargaining chips on the grand chessboard of international politics.

Married to the Throne, Not Each Other

For countless generations, royal matrimony was less about lovebirds and more about love of *land*. A king's marriage could unite empires or at least snag a nice new colony. Think of it as geopolitical Tinder: swipe right on a princess to secure an alliance and maybe a few warships. European royals in particular treated marriage as an extension of foreign policy – marriage for political, economic, or diplomatic reasons was the pattern for centuries among European rulers. The bride and groom's personal feelings weren't even on the invitation; what mattered was the merger of dynasties. Kings and queens were paired off like chess pieces to broker treaties or trade deals (Queen to King 5 – checkmate, we have a trade agreement!).

In this world, the very notion of marrying "for love" would have been scoffed at in royal circles. Love? How adorable. Monarchs had more *serious* considerations – like how many soldiers or ducats the in-laws were bringing to the table. A monarch's heart was essentially property of the state, to be given away as the ultimate diplomatic gift. If a prince's hand in marriage could pacify a rival kingdom or add a new province, then sign him up – whether or not he'd met the lucky lady. In fact, many royal spouses met for the first time literally moments before exchanging vows. There are cases of kings seeing only a portrait of their betrothed before the wedding – the 16th-century version of falling in love with someone's Instagram feed. (Henry VIII famously chose Anne of Cleves from her portrait and was sorely disappointed in person – early proof that profile pics can be misleading.)

Once wed, these couples learned quickly that *three's a crowd when one of them is an entire country*. The royal bed was often a cold and crowded place – not due to an overabundance of spouses (well, except for Henry VIII cycling through wives), but because the weight of a whole realm snuggled in between. A king and queen might physically occupy one marriage, but spiritually there was a third presence under the covers: the kingdom's interests. As one historian put it bluntly, heredity and alliance, not affection, were the pillars of royal marriage. The husband and wife's duty to dynasty meant they were effectively *married to their realms*. They woke up each day not to whisper sweet nothings to each other, but to juggle court factions and diplomatic dispatches. Little wonder that tenderness could be in short supply.

To be fair, some arranged royal matches did evolve into workable partnerships – even friendships or the occasional affection – over time. A pair might bond over the shared absurdity of their situation ("Remember how we sealed that wool trade deal by getting hitched? Pass the tea, dear."). A famous example is King Henry VII of England and Elizabeth of York. Their 1486 marriage was a political masterstroke to unite warring dynasties, and Henry hadn't even met Elizabeth beforehand. He was initially wary (imagine being nervous that your new wife might actually have a *stronger* claim to your throne – awkward!), but after meeting her, Henry VII found himself quite taken with his bride. Chronicles note that the two exchanged small gifts and grew to genuinely care for each other, providing a rare "happy ever after" in an era of cold alliances. They got lucky – literally and figuratively – but they were the exception. For most, the ideal of marrying for love was about as realistic as a dragon in the moat. Royal marriage was duty. And duty, unlike Cupid, doesn't stock up on roses and chocolates.

The consequences of this duty-above-all approach were sometimes comically grim. Passion could be so absent that producing an heir became a scheduled state chore (accompanied by uncomfortable public pressure – courtiers essentially timing the nursery arrival like sports fans awaiting a championship). If an arranged pair truly couldn't stand each other, divorce was generally off the table – so they found *creative* outlets for their misery. Some kings took mistresses as a second outlet for affection, while queens found solace in hobbies, religion, or influencing politics behind the scenes. In extreme cases, an unhappy royal spouse might be disposed of via convenient annulment or worse (looking at you, Henry VIII, with that "execute and annul" strategy). Anything was preferable to admitting that the whole political marriage concept was fundamentally flawed. Better to lop off a head or two than undermine the system, apparently.

In short, being "married to the throne" meant you weren't really expected to be married to each other in any modern sense. It was a contract between families, kingdoms – *everyone* except the two individuals saying "I do." The result was a lot of lonely queens, frustrated kings, and a trail of spectacularly dysfunctional family drama that would make today's reality TV look tame. The next time you grumble about in-laws, be glad they're not the Kingdom of France or the Holy Roman Empire demanding grandchildren. For royals of old, every marriage was an alliance first and a relationship second – if ever. And if love somehow blossomed? That was a happy coincidence, certainly nothing to plan on. After all, the crown's motto might as well have been: "*Love* is for peasants; we have policy to consider."

Strange Bedfellows (Literally)

Of course, when you marry people off for reasons of state, you're bound to get some bizarre couples. Political matchmaking wasn't concerned with compatible personalities or cozy romance – only pedigree and politics. The result? Some royal bedchambers hosted duos so oddly matched you'd think a prankster Cupid had shot the wrong people. Teenage monarchs who barely spoke the same language were thrust into conjugal cohabitation, making for very awkward palace breakfasts indeed. Picture the scene: a 15-year-old king from Country A and a 14-year-old princess from Country B sit silently as servants hover – they can't chat because his *Deutsch* and her *Français* only overlap in Latin, which they're too shy to use. Instead, they pass the marmalade in polite silence while desperately trying to recall their tutor's translation of "Could you please pass the salt?" An eyewitness to one such union of Prince Arthur of England and Catherine of Aragon noted the young couple's only common tongue was Latin – and even that didn't go smoothly, given their accents and nerves. Small wonder many of these arranged newlyweds preferred avoiding each other outside of official duties; it beat struggling through multilingual pillow talk.

Sometimes these odd pairings went beyond just language barriers. There were royal couples who instantly disliked – even loathed – one another, yet were stuck together by treaty. In such cases, the strategies for coping ranged from *polite avoidance* (separate wings of the palace and coordinating schedules so they'd rarely meet) to outright public feuding. Take the cringe-inducing marriage of Britain's Prince George (later King George IV) and Princess Caroline of Brunswick – a union arranged purely to get the playboy prince out of debt and produce an heir. The two met for the first time just days before the wedding and it was antipathy at first sight. Caroline found George repulsive and overweight; George complained Caroline was nothing like her portrait (oh, the perils of 18th-century "profile pics"!). He coped with his displeasure in classic fashion: by getting roaring drunk at their wedding. George imbided so

19

much that he spent most of his wedding night unconscious on the floor. (Caroline, noting her new husband's prone and intoxicated state, drily remarked that he'd "passed the greatest part of his bridal night under the grate, where I left him" – in other words, passed out in the fireplace.) They managed to fulfill their duty long enough to conceive a daughter – apparently on the couple of occasions George was sober enough in that first week – and then promptly split apart in mutual disgust. The Prince regent even tried to divorce Caroline years later, calling her *"the vilest wretch this world was ever cursed with"* out of pure spite. So much for wedded bliss. Their marriage became a public spectacle of *royal hate*, culminating in Caroline being literally barred from George's coronation – the doors of Westminster Abbey slammed in the poor woman's face while she banged and shouted "I am the Queen!" to no avail. You can't script a more absurd marital farce.

One infamous odd couple took the idea of *"til death do us part"* a bit too far – their union ended in a coup d'état. In 18th-century Russia, young Grand Duke Peter (the future Peter III) was married off to Princess Sophie of Anhalt-Zerbst (the future Catherine the Great) by imperial arrangement. The two teenagers had little in common: he was an immature, Prussian-raised heir with a love of toy soldiers, and she was a bright, ambitious import who quickly rebranded herself Russian. To say sparks didn't fly would be an understatement. They actively disliked each other from the get-go. Peter preferred playing with his toy army and partying, while Catherine preferred reading French philosophy and, you know, governing something. Loveless since the start of their arranged union, the pair's marriage was a disaster – awkward, cold, and increasingly hostile. Peter notoriously abandoned Catherine on their wedding night to carouse with his friends, which rather set the tone. Both soon sought companionship elsewhere (discreet infidelity was practically a job perk in such marriages). Fast forward 18 years: Peter III ascends the throne and manages to alienate just about everyone in a few short months; Catherine, politically savvy and fed up, decides she'd be a better ruler. In a dramatic turn of events, Catherine organized a coup in 1762, overthrowing her hapless husband and seizing the Russian throne for herself. Talk about marital conflict resolution! She literally *uncrowned* the man. Peter III "abdicated" (at sword-point) and conveniently died soon after, while Catherine styled herself Empress and went on to rule gloriously for decades. It's an extreme way to fix a bad marriage, but it certainly ensured no need for an awkward silver anniversary celebration. As one wry commentator noted, that particular arranged marriage was so disastrous that it ended with the wife nicknaming her spouse "former Tsar."

Such cases underscore how political pairings could turn into theater of the absurd, with real political fallout. A mismatched royal couple wasn't just tabloid fodder (though there was definitely gossip aplenty); it could trigger international incidents. If a marriage alliance went sour, alliances between their countries might fray too. When King Henry VIII annulled his politically expedient marriage to Anne of Cleves (complaining about her looks in rather ungentlemanly fashion), it embarrassed the German Duchy that sent her and nearly upended the alliance – fortunately, Anne chose to play nice and accepted a generous settlement instead of stirring trouble. In another case, when Napoleon Bonaparte divorced his true love Joséphine to marry an Austrian princess for an heir, it created such bitterness that Austria later wavered on its loyalty to Napoleon – family holidays were *tense*, to say the least. And consider the medieval saga of Isabella of Angoulême: a widowed queen whose remarriage nearly ignited civil war because her many children from the second marriage threatened to upstage the first marriage's heir. In short, arranging two strangers to wed and hoping for the best was always a gamble. Sometimes you got a power couple who tolerated each other and upheld the alliance; other times you got George and Caroline – a royal train wreck that everyone could see coming like a slow-motion carriage accident.

So how did royals cope when spouse-as-duty felt more like shackle than support? The menu of coping mechanisms included separate palaces (the deluxe version of "separate bedrooms"), icy politeness in public (gritting one's teeth through ceremonial dances), and a mutual understanding to seek companionship elsewhere as long as discretion was maintained. Many kings kept mistresses; many queens cultivated beloved confidants or advisors – anything to fill the emotional void. In extreme scenarios, they plotted against each other (Catherine wasn't the only consort with rebellious ideas; just ask Henry II's queen, Eleanor of Aquitaine, who at one point supported her sons in rebelling against their father). It's no wonder one historian quipped that behind every great royal marriage of convenience were *two people eagerly doing their own thing*. Strange bedfellows indeed – sometimes not even sharing a bed, and certainly not sharing much of a life. In the annals of arranged marriages, the absurdity and drama reached peak levels in palaces, proving that forced proximity without fondness can lead to truly deranged outcomes (coup d'état, anyone?).

When Love Upsets the Apple Cart

Given this backdrop of dutiful but often dreary unions, imagine the shock when occasionally a royal bucked the system and said, "To blazes with alliance – I'm marrying for love!" Such an idea was the ultimate scandal, a veritable hand grenade rolled into the royal court's tea party. In traditions where marrying for strategic gain was gospel, a monarch insisting on personal affection was seen as either *deranged or dangerously modern*. Was this young royal touched by madness, or simply ahead of their time? Reactions varied from gasps and fainting fits among courtiers to full-blown constitutional crises.

One of the most famous instances of Cupid's arrow clashing with the Crown's agenda came in 1936. King Edward VIII of Britain fell head-over-heels for Wallis Simpson – an American divorcée with, ahem, two living ex-husbands – and decided he *would* marry her, come hell or high politics. The British establishment promptly lost its collective mind. Here was the King-Emperor of a global empire proposing to marry a twice-divorced commoner, *and* an American to boot, in an era when royals weren't even allowed to marry Catholics or divorcées. The Church, the government, his own family – everyone was against it. The press whispered about her past and his "derangement." It became a constitutional crisis that rocked the monarchy. In the end, love (or infatuation) upended the apple cart entirely: Edward VIII renounced his throne – the ultimate mic-drop for love. In a radio broadcast that stunned listeners worldwide, he confessed he could not carry on as King "without the help and support of the woman I love". And just like that, Britain got a new king (Edward's stammering younger brother, George VI) and a lasting cautionary tale. Edward married Wallis in exile; the monarchy survived, but the episode proved that even the crown wasn't immune to a lovestruck heart willing to burn down a kingdom's expectations. It was perhaps the most dramatic example of *marrying for love, royal edition*, and it showed how fiercely tradition would fight back. Many in Britain viewed Edward's choice as selfish and reckless – evidence that pursuing personal happiness at the expense of duty was borderline treasonous. Deranged or romantic genius? History still debates it, but the couple did stay together for life (living out a rather bored, cocktail-soaked existence in France, far from any throne).

Not every love match in royal history led to abdication, but most caused a fair bit of drama. Often, it was younger royals – spares to the throne, widowed princesses, etc. – who dared to break protocol. In the Tudor era, for example, a few high-born ladies shocked the court by marrying men well below their station purely for love, incurring royal wrath and scandal. These marriages were usually followed by a lot of tut-tutting about how *romantic love was no basis for matrimony*. (For context, in the 1500s "marrying down" could literally get you disinherited. One Spanish princess in England, Catherine of Valois, had to keep her second marriage to a mere knight secret for as long as possible, because a Queen marrying a commoner was political dynamite in 15th-century Europe.) When Queen Victoria, as a young monarch in the 1840s, chose to marry her cousin Prince Albert, it was actually a bit revolutionary – not because

Albert was beneath her (he was a prince, if a relatively minor one), but because she married for genuine love and attraction. Her advisors had lined up various candidates, but Victoria insisted on Albert because she truly adored him. The courtiers sighed in relief that at least Albert had royal blood; otherwise the match might've been squashed as "deranged." Even so, Victoria's deep love for Albert (and her open grief when he died) introduced a novel idea: that a reigning sovereign *could* sincerely love their spouse. It made her more human in her people's eyes. Still, many at the time found it all a bit sentimental for a queen.

A more scandalous love match occurred when a royal was willing to marry someone deemed far beneath their station. In the late 19th century, Austria's Crown Prince Rudolf fell in love with a Baron's daughter (below his rank) – that ended in tragedy at Mayerling. A happier example: in 1900, Archduke Franz Ferdinand of Austria (heir presumptive to the throne) stubbornly insisted on marrying Sophie Chotek, a lady-in-waiting with no royal title. The Emperor allowed it only as a morganatic marriage – meaning Sophie and their kids would never inherit the throne – essentially a royal demotion for love. They married, reportedly a true love match, and by all accounts were devoted to each other. The court, however, ostracized poor Sophie at every turn (she often couldn't sit near her husband at official banquets due to her lower rank – talk about awkward). Their story ended tragically when both were assassinated in 1914, but in terms of our theme, they proved a point: a royal willing to *risk it all* for love might keep their head and their crown (Franz kept his position, Sophie just didn't share it fully) – yet they would pay a social price. The "apple cart" of tradition was thoroughly upset; the Habsburg elite never forgave Franz Ferdinand for valuing personal happiness over dynastic duty. Some historians even suggest his isolation at court contributed to the lack of support that led to his fateful trip to Sarajevo. Love had literally world-shaking consequences here (World War I, anyone?).

Less dire but still dramatic are the many princes and princesses who in the 20th century began pushing back on arranged expectations. Princess Margaret (sister of Queen Elizabeth II) wanted to marry a divorced commoner in the 1950s – the establishment basically told her "Nope, not allowed," and she had to give him up, illustrating how recently the old rules still held. By the 1960s, though, things start to shift. A young King of Norway, Harald, fell in love with a commoner (Sonja) and insisted he would have no one else; he even told his father he'd remain unmarried (leaving the dynasty without an heir) if he couldn't have her. The Norwegian court yielded, and Harald married Sonja in 1968 – today they're the beloved King and Queen of Norway. Scandalous? Back then, yes – a true commoner as Queen – but love scored a victory. Likewise, Japan's then-Crown Prince Akihito broke precedent by marrying a lovely commoner, Michiko, in 1959. The press called it a "Cinderella" story; traditionalists grumbled. Michiko, now Empress Emerita, faced intense pressure (legend has it stress rendered her mute for a time), but their marriage proved enduring. Each such instance chipped away at the notion that royals must marry only their own kind.

And guess what? Sometimes these love matches turned out to be the happiest of all – or at least no more disastrous than the arranged train wrecks they could have had. Queen Victoria and Prince Albert, despite some marital spats, had a famously devoted marriage and nine children. The current British monarch's parents, Queen Elizabeth II and Prince Philip, married for love (yes, he was a Greek/Danish prince, but basically a stranger until they met as teens and sparks flew) and they enjoyed a 73-year partnership – full of love, respect, and the usual bickering, but certainly a solid team. It's as if when royals actually choose someone they fancy, they stand a fighting chance of a decent marriage, politics be damned. On the other hand, loveless arranged pairings were often *guaranteed* misery. As our examples show, marrying for duty gave us civil wars, beheadings, coups, and doors slammed in faces. Marrying for love gave us…occasionally a resigned king and some gossip, but arguably fewer political corpses. Over time, even the stodgiest royal handlers had to concede that a content monarch might govern more effectively than one trapped in a toxic union. By the late 20th century, the writing was on the wall (probably scrawled by a rebellious princess with a lipstick): the heart wants what it wants, and even a crown can't trump chemistry forever.

From Contract to Connection

Fast-forward to today's royal landscape, and you'll see a *mostly* changed scene – one that might astonish our Ancien Régime ancestors. Modern princes and princesses are far more likely to marry a college sweetheart, a commoner next door, or even a celebrity, embracing the radical 21st-century concept that maybe – just maybe – marrying someone you actually love is a good idea. The transformation from rigid dynastic contracts to personal love matches has been gradual and not without stumbles, but it has undeniably made monarchies more relatable to the public (not to mention more bearable for the royals themselves).

In the 1700s and 1800s, romantic love started gaining cultural importance (blame those poets and novelists), and slowly royals followed suit. By the mid-20th century, arranged royal marriages in Europe had virtually vanished. These days, if a king announced he was marrying a princess he'd never met for a treaty, people would assume they'd stumbled into a time warp or a particularly outlandish episode of *The Crown*. Instead, we have examples like Britain's Prince William marrying Catherine "Kate" Middleton – his university classmate and a bona fide commoner from a middle-class family. A few centuries ago, Kate's lack of royal blood would have been a deal-breaker (the poor girl's ancestors were miners and merchants, gasp!). But in 2011 it was hailed as a refreshing modernization. Courtiers touted the match as *"breaking with tradition"* and making the monarchy *more accessible* by bringing in new blood. Indeed, the British royal family's willingness to welcome commoners into its ranks is a very recent development – but it's now standard practice. Prince Harry followed suit by marrying Meghan Markle, an American actress of mixed race – something that would have been unthinkable a few generations back. Other European monarchies have similar stories: the Crown Princess of Sweden wed her personal trainer; the King of the Netherlands married an Argentine banker he met at a party (she didn't even know he was a prince at first – imagine finding *that* out on date number two!); the King of Spain married a news anchor; Jordan's King married a Palestinian commoner (Queen Rania, now globally admired); even the heir to the Japanese throne, Princess Mako, recently married her college sweetheart (a commoner), *knowing she'd lose her royal status as a result*. Around the world, royal romances increasingly read like modern love stories rather than chapters of a diplomatic almanac.

This evolution was not smooth sailing. Traditionalists in every royal court initially fretted that marrying "out" would dilute the bloodline or undermine mystique. There have been murmurs of discontent from old-guard aristocrats about "suitable" matches. When then-Crown Prince Naruhito of Japan married Masako Owada (a career diplomat from no aristocratic lineage) in 1993, the Imperial Household Agency nearly had a meltdown — Masako herself famously likened joining the Imperial family to entering a convent under intense public scrutiny. In Britain, the tabloids and some insiders had a field day with Prince Harry's choice of Meghan — a divorced American, echoing the Wallis Simpson saga but with a happier outcome (no abdication this time, though the couple did eventually step back from royal duties, proving modern love can still ruffle feathers). Even earlier, when Prince Charles married Lady Diana Spencer in 1981, it was hailed as a fairy-tale — but notably, Diana *was* an aristocrat (if technically a commoner). The pressure for heirs to pick someone "appropriate" lingered late into the 20th century. Charles's true love, Camilla, was initially deemed unsuitable, contributing to a tragic royal love triangle that played out in global headlines. Only years later, after much heartache, did Charles finally marry Camilla. By then, the public and palace had come around to the idea that happiness mattered more than old protocols. The Queen's blessing of that union in 2005 symbolized how far things had come: a future king marrying for love, even if it meant bending bygone rules (Camilla was divorced, which decades earlier would have barred her).

Today's young royals are expected – even encouraged – to find their own partners, with personal compatibility foremost. It's almost completely flipped from the age when marriages were arranged by governments. In fact, one could argue modern royal marriages serve a different "strategic" purpose: not forging alliances between nations, but forging alliances with the public. A relatable love story can endear a royal couple to the populace more than any treaty ever could. The fairy-tale narrative of a prince and his everyday love is PR gold for monarchies trying to stay relevant. When Prince William brought Kate (now Catherine, Duchess of Cambridge) into the fold, the monarchy's approval ratings got a noticeable boost – a popular commoner bride made the ancient institution feel fresh and accessible. The same dynamic is seen elsewhere – when Crown Princess Victoria of Sweden married Daniel (a gym owner), Swedes celebrated the idea that their future queen followed her heart and married "one of us." Modern monarchies have found that letting royals marry for love hasn't caused the sky to fall; rather, it humanizes them. People like to see that even those born to privilege prefer a partner who gives them the *warm fuzzies* over one who simply has the right pedigree.

That's not to say the collision of centuries-old expectations with 21st-century romance is without hiccups. Tension can still arise when duty and love tug in different directions. For example, Japan's Princess Mako, as noted, had to relinquish her royal title and allowance to marry her sweetheart – a reminder that some royal houses still have strict rules (in Japan, princesses who marry commoners must leave the imperial family). The British royals, while embracing love matches, have had to weather the fallout when those matches clash with tradition or media scrutiny (the Harry and Meghan saga being the prime example of tradition vs. personal choice vs. relentless public gaze). And whenever a royal marries a commoner, there's the inevitable learning curve for the newcomer: the do's and don'ts of palace life, the antiquated protocols, and sometimes a skeptical courtiers' clique. It's essentially the plot of every Hallmark movie where the prince's fiancée has to learn which fork to use and curtsy correctly – except in real life, getting it wrong can cause a minor press frenzy. Yet, by and large, the trend is clear: the age of marrying purely for dynasty is over (at least in most places), and the era of marrying for connection is here. In a historical blink of an eye, we went from *"You will marry this foreign duke's daughter because the state requires it"* to *"You can marry whomever you love – we trust you to choose well (just maybe avoid convicted felons, please)."*

And believe it or not, even the bluest of blue bloods are finding that love doesn't dilute their royal aura – if anything, it enhances it. Watching a prince marry his longtime girlfriend (instead of a stranger of proper rank) or a queen consort swap an arranged match for her true love after a long wait (looking at Camilla, finally getting her Charles) makes these exalted figures oddly *normal*. They become people who worry about work-life balance and in-laws, just like us – except their "work" is national duty and their in-laws are, well, the entire nation. The public response to this humanization has generally been positive. Crowds cheer for commoner brides and grooms; fairy-tale metaphors abound in media coverage. It's as if everyone is relieved that royalty have hearts that beat, not just protocols to follow. One could even argue that the longevity of certain monarchies into the 21st century owes something to this adaptability in the marriage department. A monarch who marries for love likely has a more stable home life, which can translate to better performance of duties – or at least fewer scandalous distractions.

In the end, the journey from "contract to connection" in royal marriages shows an institution bending (sometimes kicking and screaming) toward the norms of common humanity. Arranged alliances gave way, gradually, to love matches – and monarchies did not crumble. Instead, they often gained a bit of sparkle and sincerity. Even the term "royal couple" means something different now: it conjures images of genuine partnership rather than a stern-faced pair bound by obligation. Modern royal spouses hold hands in public, share little inside jokes at state events, and even hug their kids on camera – gestures that would have been unthinkably informal for Queen Victoria's generation. The cameras may stop rolling, but today we suspect that behind palace doors, many kings and queens are doing something radical: living relatively normal married lives (or as normal as you can get when your house is literally called a palace). They bicker over what's for dinner, tease each other, support each other at tough times – you know, *marriage.*

It only took a few millennia, but royals have learned what common folk knew all along: marriage is hard enough under the best circumstances, so it helps if you actually like – or dare we say love – your partner. And if you can achieve that, even a gilded cage can start to feel like a home. The blue bloods can indeed get the warm fuzzies, and when they do, it's a win for the couple and the crown alike. After all, a throne for two is a lot more comfortable when both seats are occupied by choice, not by coercion. And if any traditionalists are still clutching their pearls about it, well, they can take comfort in one thing: even in a love marriage, the decorative china is probably still safe – unless, of course, a modern Catherine the Great decides to start flinging plates instead of launching coups. But hey, that's marriage – royal or not.

Chapter 3

Pillow Politics – Power Plays in the Boudoir

R oyal bedrooms aren't just for sleeping – historically, they've doubled as unofficial strategy rooms and war rooms. When the crown comes off and the silk nightcap goes on, a king or queen isn't simply drifting to dreamland; they're often getting an earful of advice (or demands) from the spouse on the pillow next to them. If you thought boardroom politics were intense, imagine the boardroom being your bedroom with your partner as your top advisor. Indeed, from ancient palaces to modern estates, some of the most crucial decisions were made under the covers, with pillow talk literally shaping the course of kingdoms. In this chapter, we pull back the brocade bed curtains to explore how royal couples have negotiated power, hatched plots, betrayed each other, or teamed up as allies—all in the privacy of their boudoir. It's a realm where love, power, and intrigue entwine as tightly as a pair of monogrammed bedsheets.

The Power Behind the Throne (Is in Bed)

They say behind every great king is a queen rolling her eyes – and then rolling up her sleeves once they're alone. In royal history, the true power behind the throne was often lying beside it in a silk gown or embroidered pajamas. The royal bedchamber served as a second office, where whispered suggestions could carry more weight than proclamations in the throne room. After all, who needs a prime minister or a privy council when your spouse has your ear (quite literally) on the pillow every night?

From ancient empresses to modern consorts, many a ruler was guided by a better half with a sharp wit and a knack for strategy. Consider the Byzantine Emperor Justinian and his formidable wife Empress Theodora in the 6th century – a power couple if ever there was one. Think of them as the Jay-Z and Beyoncé of their day, but with an empire to run instead of a music label. When a violent revolt (the Nika riots) threatened their throne, Justinian was all set to flee the capital in panic. It was Theodora who reputedly put her foot down and told him in no uncertain terms that she'd rather die an Empress than live as a commoner. "Purple makes a fine burial shroud," she supposedly declared, referring to the royal purple robes. In modern terms, she basically said, *"We're not quitting, honey. We've come too far to give up now."* Her steely midnight counsel stiffened Justinian's spine, and he ended up crushing the rebellion and keeping his crown – all thanks to a dose of pillow-delivered tough love. Talk about bedside motivational speaking!

Across cultures, royal spouses have often been the ultimate back-channel advisers. In the Ottoman Empire, Sultan Suleiman the Magnificent had his beloved wife Hürrem Sultan (known in the West as Roxelana) as his confidante. Hürrem started as a concubine and broke tradition by becoming Suleiman's official wife, gaining unprecedented influence. Once she had his ear (and his heart), she didn't hesitate to offer political input. At night, she wasn't just asking how his day went – more likely she was urging him to deal with that troublesome vizier or to consider which of his sons should inherit the throne. She even convinced Suleiman to have his most promising heir (his eldest son by another wife) executed on dubious charges, all to secure her own son's succession. Pillow talk with a body count, indeed! Who says a queen's whispers can't change the world? In this case, Hürrem's murmured counsel altered the course of an empire's future.

Even in more recent royal history, the spousal influence in private is the stuff of legend. Queen Victoria of Britain was the monarch, but her husband Prince Albert was often the power behind the throne – or should we say behind the bedroom door. Victoria adored Albert and relied on his guidance in governing. Night after night, they would discuss matters of state by the fire. Albert, never officially king, nonetheless became her chief adviser and unofficial co-ruler in many ways. He helped refine policies, championed modernization and science, and even managed the royal children (which in a way was its own political challenge in a dynasty). One might imagine Victoria venting about some prime minister, and Albert gently suggesting, "Perhaps support that new railway initiative, dear; it'll make us look quite progressive." By morning, the Queen's mind would be made up – and coincidentally it often aligned with Albert's viewpoint. Even in the 20th century, Queen Elizabeth II's husband Prince Philip was known to offer her the frank advice no one else dared – a modern echo of the old pillow-power dynamic. A consort might not hold official office, but in the royal bedchamber they could speak with an honesty and candor that sometimes swayed the course set by the crown. In short, the marital bedroom has long been an incubator for royal decision-making. Free from eavesdropping ministers and flattering yes-men, a king or queen could hear the one voice who would tell them the truth (or at least a truth skewed by love and ambition). The bedchamber's whispers often trumped the council chamber's debates. Next time you picture a monarch issuing orders, remember that those commands may have been rehearsed in a much cozier setting, with only the royal pajamas in attendance. The real power behind the throne might just have been tucked in beside it, murmuring ideas that shaped history.

Conspiracies by Candlelight

Of course, not all pillow talk was benign or filled with loving counsel. Sometimes those midnight whispers took a turn toward the dark and devious. It sounds like something out of Shakespeare – think Lady Macbeth urging on her husband – but these were real royals doing real plotting. Picture a king and queen propped up on overstuffed pillows in their grand canopy bed, candles flickering low, as they softly scheme to remove a rival or settle a political score. This is marital bonding, royal edition: plotting by candlelight. Two heads on the same plush pillow, dreaming up someone else's downfall. Cozy, isn't it?

History offers plenty of real cases where bedtime chats veered into treacherous territory. For instance, Empress Catherine the Great of Russia quite literally turned pillow talk into a coup d'état. Catherine didn't earn the title "the Great" by meekly staying under the covers. In 1762, after years of enduring her husband Tsar Peter III's buffoonery (he was immature, unpopular, and more interested in toy soldiers than ruling),

Catherine decided *enough was enough*. Along with a few close confidants (some of whom might have shared more than just political strategy in her boudoir), she plotted to overthrow her own spouse. In the early hours of a summer morning, Catherine put her plan into action. Legend has it she was awakened at dawn by an ally warning that their plot was at risk of being discovered. Without hesitating, Catherine threw on a uniform, mounted a horse, and rallied the Imperial Guards to her side. By breakfast time, her dear hubby Peter was out of a job – forced to abdicate – and Catherine had proclaimed herself Empress of Russia. (Peter, for his part, didn't survive to dinner; let's just say "mysterious circumstances" befell him shortly after.) The whole episode was essentially a palace coup launched from the bedroom. Catherine's late-night scheming literally changed who sat on the throne by sunrise.

She wasn't the only queen to plot against a king. Jump back a few centuries to medieval England, and meet Queen Isabella of France, who earned the nickname "She-Wolf of France" for her formidable, not-so-wifely behavior. Married to King Edward II of England, Isabella had a miserable time – her husband infamously neglected her and infuriated his barons with his favoritism toward certain courtiers. After years of feeling ignored and disrespected, Isabella chose the nuclear option. In 1326 she joined forces with her lover, Roger Mortimer, and led an invasion *against her own husband*. Yes, you read that right: she raised an army, marched on England, and sent King Edward running for his life. By the following year, Edward II had been deposed (and later met a very grim fate, if the lurid legends are to be believed), and Isabella was effectively ruling on behalf of her young son. One imagines that at some point during a particularly frosty marital bedtimes, Isabella might have stared at the ceiling and thought, "I could do a better job than him." And then she went out and proved it. Talk about taking "relationship problems" to a whole new level.

Not every seditious whisper was aimed at the spouse, of course. Sometimes the king and queen conspired together as a villainous tag-team against *someone else*. A royal couple might bond over a shared enemy – perhaps a too-powerful advisor or an inconvenient relative standing in their way. Picture them snuggled under the blankets, hatching a plan to oust that pesky prime minister by morning. *"Darling, what shall we do about that scheming duke?" "Hmm, maybe invite him on a nice hunt and arrange for a little 'accident'."* (Ah, nothing spices up pillow talk like a hint of premeditated treachery.) Whether plotting together or against one another, these candlelit conspiracies made the royal boudoir as dangerous as any war room. The same bed that hosted tender whispers by night could see a dagger drawn before dawn. Little wonder that savvy monarchs learned to sleep with one eye open. After all, who better to betray you than the person who knows your every secret and sleeps an inch from your throat? In this arena, the line between loving confidant and lethal co-conspirator was thin indeed. One minute you're sharing a goose-down duvet; the next, you're sharing state secrets and scheming somebody's demise. It's marital intimacy, royal-style – heavy on intrigue, light on innocence. The moral for any monarch? Keep your friends close, and your spouse closer… and make sure the bedtime conversation stays on the *right* side of treason.

Sleeping with the Enemy (Literally)

When royal romance curdled into suspicion, the bedchamber could become a battlefield. Kings and queens who once whispered sweet nothings might start sleeping with one eye open, fearing the very person beside them. It's hard to blame them – when the stakes are life, death, and empire, trust is a fragile thing.

A famous cautionary tale comes from the 12th century. King Henry II of England and Queen Eleanor of Aquitaine were the original power couple for years – until they weren't. After over a decade of marriage (and many children together), their relationship soured amid political tensions and Henry's blatant infidelities. Eleanor actually went so far as to encourage their sons to rebel against Henry. In 1173 this family feud exploded: the young princes raised armies against dear old Dad, apparently with Mom's secret encouragement. Henry II crushed the rebellion and, furious at his wife's betrayal, promptly had Eleanor locked up. Not for a week or a month – for sixteen years. That's possibly the longest "grounding" in history. The legendary Eleanor spent the remainder of Henry's reign confined in one castle or another, put under house arrest by her own husband. Talk about a marital timeout! Henry decided he simply couldn't trust his queen not to plot against him again, so he kept her under lock and key. It was an extreme (and extremely dysfunctional) example of spousal distrust, and a stark reminder that even the mightiest royal couples could end up as bitter enemies.

In many royal courts, paranoia became a third party in the marriage. Queens might secretly read the king's correspondence, searching for signs of betrayal or evidence of yet another mistress. Kings, for their part, often employed tasters to sip their wine and stationed guards in their bedchamber – not just to thwart assassins in the palace halls, but sometimes to keep an eye on their own "beloved" spouse. One medieval monarch reportedly even refused to sleep in the same room as his queen once whispers of poison started swirling. Nothing says "I love you" like posting a few guards at the bedroom door and having your meal tested for toxins by an unlucky servant. In the royal world, a healthy dose of mutual suspicion was often just part of the marriage package.

And of course, there were those unions that ended in outright terror. Henry VIII of England provides the ultimate example of a spouse you definitely couldn't trust (and who definitely didn't trust you). When this Tudor king's faith in a wife evaporated, so did her head – quite literally. Henry accused two of his six wives of adultery and treason (charges that ranged from trumped-up to entirely baseless) and had them executed. Anne Boleyn, his second queen, found herself arrested and beheaded in 1536 after Henry decided she had been unfaithful. (More likely, he was just desperate for a male heir and needed to swap out wives – but that's a story for another chapter.) A few years later, his fifth wife Catherine Howard met the same fate, on similar accusations. For Henry, "'til death do us part" was less a romantic vow and more a convenient exit strategy. Small wonder that by the end of his reign, any woman married to him probably slept uneasily, knowing a mere whiff of scandal could send her to the chopping block. In Henry's court, the matrimonial bed truly became a danger zone.

All these episodes drive home one point: a royal marriage without trust was a ticking time bomb. Imagine living under the same gilded roof and sharing the same bed, yet constantly wondering if your partner might betray or even eliminate you. It's a nerve-wracking way to spend your nights (and days). Sharing a crown turned out to be even harder than sharing a closet. The next time you feel a pang of jealousy or doubt in your own humble relationship, be grateful it likely won't end with someone locked in a tower or sent to the block. In the palace, those were very real possibilities when you were literally sleeping with the enemy.

Allies or Adversaries?

So were royal husbands and wives typically a dynamic duo, or more like dueling monarchs? The answer varied wildly. Some marriages became the ultimate tag-team of power, while others devolved into a constant tug-of-war over the throne.

On the bright side, take King Ferdinand of Aragon and Queen Isabella of Castile. Their union in the late 15th century literally created the foundation of a united Spain, and they genuinely worked in tandem. They shared a vision (finish the Reconquista, strengthen their realms, and even sponsor a certain Christopher Columbus on his gamble of a voyage) and they stuck together through it all. If one had a doubt, the other offered resolve. They were by all accounts a true power couple — two monarchs in partnership, making decisions together and presenting a united front. No petty rivalry there. In fact, England even had a later example of a joint monarchy: William III and Mary II, in the 1680s, ruled as co-sovereigns and by all accounts navigated the arrangement without major marital strife (tragically cut short when Mary died young). Ferdinand and Isabella, for their part, earned the nickname "the Catholic Monarchs" for their united efforts. A marital high-five is definitely deserved for that duo.

On the other end of the spectrum, consider Mary, Queen of Scots and her second husband, Lord Darnley – a textbook case of a royal marriage imploding spectacularly. What began as a promising alliance quickly turned into a nightmare. Darnley was arrogant, petty, and prone to violence. He even had Mary's favorite secretary brutally murdered in her presence, which is one way to ruin date night. Mary grew to loathe him. Less than two years into the marriage, Darnley's house mysteriously blew up one night – and he ended up dead in the orchard, very clearly murdered. Many suspected Mary knew more about this "accident" than she let on (her swift remarriage to the chief suspect, Lord Bothwell, didn't do her reputation any favors). In short, their royal household was basically a civil war in miniature, complete with literal explosions. Definitely no teamwork there.

The lesson from these tales? Two strong-willed royals in one marriage can be either each other's greatest asset or each other's worst liability. When they pulled together as true partners, they could achieve world-changing feats. But when they turned against each other, it was chaos for the couple – and often for the realm as well. It's darkly comic in hindsight: a king and queen battling it out like an epic domestic squabble with a crown on the line. For them, though, it was deadly serious business. Thankfully, most of us will never have to worry that a spat with our spouse might trigger a national crisis. So next time you and your significant other have a minor disagreement, be glad it won't start a civil war – and take a page from these royals: try cooperation before reaching for the poison goblet, okay?

Chapter 4

Battle Royal – When Spouses Go to War (Figuratively... Usually)

In the grand theatre of royalty, marriage isn't all fairy-tale waltzes and harmonious co-rule. When kings and queens shut the palace doors, they can squabble like any couple – except their tiffs might influence whole kingdoms. Imagine a domestic argument over dinner plans that ends with armies mobilizing. Welcome to the Battle Royal, where royal spouses go to war (figuratively... usually) in a clash of egos, titles, and tempers. In this chapter, we unveil the secret marital battles of kings and queens – with a wink and a nudge – to see how royal couples really live when the cameras stop rolling. Along the way, we'll draw some parallels to our modern celebrity and political power couples, because, let's face it, the antics of the palace aren't so different from the drama on reality TV (just with more crowns and fewer Instagram followers).

Who Wears the Crown Tonight?

Sure, one spouse in a royal marriage might *technically* outrank the other – but behind closed doors, hierarchy isn't always clear-cut. In private chambers, the question of "Who's in charge here?" could get, well, awkward. It turns out that playing *second fiddle* doesn't come naturally to people used to being the star of the show. Think of a royal marriage as a sort of medieval *power couple* dynamic: King vs. Queen – Dawn of

Domestic Justice. The formal protocol might say one is sovereign and the other is consort, but after hours it's often a toss-up who *really* calls the shots.

Take Mary, Queen of Scots and her ill-fated husband Lord Darnley for example. Mary was the anointed Queen regnant of Scotland, undeniably the boss on paper. Yet Darnley, a king consort with a *serious* entitlement complex, wasn't content polishing his wife's crown. He demanded the Crown Matrimonial – essentially insisting on being declared co-sovereign and continuing to rule if Mary died. Mary refused to grant him this coveted status, a denial which Darnley took *very* personally. It's the 16th-century version of a celebrity husband demanding equal billing on the marquee – and throwing a tantrum when he doesn't get it. Their domestic life descended into chaos: Darnley sulked and schemed, at one point even joining a band of rebellious nobles and dramatically *helping murder* Mary's favorite Italian secretary in front of the pregnant queen (talk about taking "who wears the crown" too literally!). Mary and Darnley's marriage became so toxic that it could rival anything on modern tabloid covers. In fact, if social media existed then, we'd probably have #TeamMary vs #TeamDarnley trending for months on end. Darnley's insistence on being *the man in charge* led to a spiral of distrust and betrayal – culminating in his own suspicious demise when his house blew up and he was found strangled in a garden. (Note to self: if you ever feel frustrated that your spouse isn't respecting your authority, maybe don't plot against a reigning queen – it tends to end poorly.)

On a lighter note, picture a contemporary power couple like Beyoncé and Jay-Z deciding who runs the household each night. By day she's Queen Bey and he's hip-hop royalty, but maybe at home they bicker over who controls the remote. Now crank that up to royal intensity: in some palaces, kings and queens actually argued over who got to make appointments to high office or who had the final say on state policy, rather than whose turn it was to take out the trash. The stakes were a *tad* higher. In one corner, a monarch raised to expect total deference; in the other, a consort who might also be of royal blood or simply strong-willed and used to getting their way. When both halves of a couple have a claim to authority, the domestic power dynamic becomes a chess match. Will the king pull rank, or will the queen manipulate events from behind the throne? Sometimes even the courtiers had no clue. There have been courts where, after a royal dinner, ministers genuinely didn't know whether to follow the orders of His Majesty or listen to Her Majesty's wishes instead. The question of "Who wears the crown tonight?" had *literal* consequences – and occasionally, everyone's answer was different.

One amusing example of blurred hierarchy comes from the marriage of Queen Mary I of England and Prince Philip of Spain. Mary was the ruling queen, and Philip was ostensibly brought in as king consort – a partnership of two monarchs from different realms. In theory Mary outranked Philip in England, but Philip expected to be treated as *every bit her equal*. The English, however, were not keen to let a foreign husband take control. Parliament went so far as to stipulate that while Philip could be called "King", he had almost no independent power; he couldn't appoint officials willy-nilly or drag England into wars for Spain. The result? A marriage contract that basically said "Welcome, Philip, you can sit at the head of the table, but don't you dare try to drive this ship." Behind palace doors, one can imagine the ego clashes. It's like a modern political marriage where one partner is a head of state and the other is also a high-powered leader – say, if two presidents married and had to figure out who gets the Oval Office desk. (Looking at you, hypothetical Clinton-Clinton White House, which thankfully we never quite had – though some joked Bill and Hillary *did* operate as co-presidents for a time.) In Mary and Philip's case, their evenings might have featured debates not unlike a couple arguing over a GPS route: Mary insisting on the English way of doing things, Philip confident the Spanish way is superior. Who ultimately wore the crown at night? Probably Mary (it was *her* realm), but Philip certainly tried to tip the balance. The ambiguity in their hierarchy even sparked a rebellion by English nobles worried Philip would dominate – a rebellion Mary quashed while pointedly reminding everyone she, the Queen, was "wedded to the realm" first and husband second. Awkward.

All these regal domestic squabbles teach a simple lesson: titles don't automatically translate to *domestic* authority. A king at court might be a henpecked husband in private, or a queen in parliament might quietly defer to her prince consort at home – or vice versa. The interplay of pride, love, and power makes royal marriages delightfully unpredictable. So next time you see a royal couple waving serenely from a balcony, remember: once the cameras turn off, it might be time for King vs. Queen: Dawn of Domestic Justice, Part II – hopefully featuring nothing more perilous than a witty repartee over who's in charge of the castle keys tonight.

Egos and Empire

Put two people under one gilded roof when *both* are used to deference and control, and you've got a recipe for epic marital showdowns. A king and queen each accustomed to getting their way can produce "too many monarchs in the kitchen." When royal egos collide, the disputes don't stay trivial – they escalate to kingdom-shaking proportions. Think of those Hollywood power couples where both are A-list stars; the fights can be fiery because neither is used to backing down. Now imagine that with actual armies at their disposal. In this section, we revisit some legendary spousal showdowns where personal pride and political authority became so intertwined that *entire realms* felt the fallout. Sometimes one spouse simply refused to play the supporting role – even if tradition and everyone else insisted they should. The result? Marital strife that would put Brad and Angelina's breakup to shame (Team Jolie and Team Pitt have nothing on Team King vs. Team Queen).

One of the most famous examples is the stormy partnership of King Henry II of England and Queen Eleanor of Aquitaine. Henry II was a formidable monarch – energetic, autocratic, used to absolute control. Eleanor, for her part, was *no ordinary queen*: she had been Duchess of Aquitaine in her own right (and a former Queen of France to boot). Eleanor was intelligent, outspoken, and every bit as accustomed to ruling as Henry. Neither was inclined to bow to the other's will. For years they managed a functional partnership, but as time went on, Henry's ego and

Eleanor's pride clashed spectacularly. The royal couple argued not just over household or personal matters, but over power – how to wield it, and who should wield it. Matters came to a head when Eleanor, fed up with Henry's overbearing style and perhaps his extramarital dalliances, egged on their sons to rebel against their father. Yes, you read that right: the Queen encouraged a family insurrection. In 1173, their three eldest sons – young princes with their own chips on their shoulders – rose in revolt against King Dad, and Queen Mom sided with the boys! Suddenly the royal marriage dispute wasn't just whispered sniping in the castle corridors; it was civil war. Talk about taking "domestic disagreement" to a whole new level. The whole kingdom effectively split into factions, with some barons loyal to the King and others secretly (or openly) supporting the Queen and rebel princes. It was a medieval version of a nasty divorce where the kids actually join one parent's lawsuit against the other – except with knights and siege weapons involved. Henry II ultimately crushed the rebellion. The *very* angry king, not known for his gentle temper, swiftly imprisoned Eleanor for her role in the uprising. (He basically put the Queen in time-out… for 16 years. That's one long marital cooling-off period.) This legendary showdown shows how personal slights – Henry's refusal to share power, Eleanor's refusal to be sidelined – turned into political earthquakes. Pride and authority were so tangled that a family argument nearly tore an empire apart. One imagines Henry and Eleanor's relationship counseling session: "I feel like you don't respect my autonomy." "Well, you raised an army against me, dear!" It makes the average counseling session seem quaint.

Henry and Eleanor weren't the only regals to let ego drive them to extremes. History is full of couples who could not abide being number two. Some kings married strong queens and then struggled to tolerate their influence; some queens married kings and chafed at being expected to just smile and wave. When both individuals see themselves as *natural leaders*, the result can be downright explosive. Consider the case of the Ottoman Sultan Suleiman the Magnificent and his brilliant wife Hurrem Sultan (Roxelana). Suleiman ruled a vast empire and was used to being the center of the universe – "Magnificent" wasn't exactly a nickname suggesting a humble personality. Hurrem, however, was extraordinarily ambitious and intelligent. She wasn't about to remain confined to the harem doing embroidery. Over time, Suleiman broke with tradition and elevated Hurrem to be his official wife and close advisor, which scandalized the old guard. The more power Hurrem gained, the more friction she caused with others at court – including Suleiman's once-heir-apparent, his eldest son by another wife. Hurrem wanted her own son to inherit, so (allegedly) she convinced Suleiman to remove the rival heir. The ensuing father-son clash (with Hurrem's whisperings in Suleiman's ear) ended with the execution of that son, splitting the court into factions supportive of Hurrem's faction vs. the traditionalists. It was essentially a *palace faction war* spurred by a wife who refused the passive role. While Suleiman and Hurrem's personal bond remained strong (they genuinely loved each other, making them an *effective* if ruthless team), their story shows how a powerful queen's ego and a powerful king's authority can create turmoil even as they cooperate. It's reminiscent of a CEO power couple in a company: if the husband is the official CEO but the wife is the brilliant COO who starts making big decisions, pretty soon the boardroom is full of whispering factions — "Who's really running things?" In an empire, those boardroom whispers become life-and-death intrigues.

We also have more genteel examples — cases where egos clashed but compromise was eventually found (we'll get to those in the next section). But before we move on, it's worth noting that whenever marital disputes escalated among royals, *everyone* had to pick a side. Courtiers, generals, even common folk would align with either the King's party or the Queen's party. It was like a massive medieval version of a Twitter feud, but instead of hashtags, they had banners and battle cries. (Imagine being a medieval peasant muttering, "Ugh, I'm so over this royal drama," as two factions ride off to battle because His and Her Majesties can't sort out their power issues.)

Modern celebrity and political couples rarely raise armies when they fight (thank goodness), but the essence isn't so different. Think of the brief period when rumors swirled about a tug-of-war between the influence of a U.S. President and his First Lady — for instance, whispers that Nancy Reagan was consulting astrologers and influencing Ronnie's schedule, or speculations that Hillary Clinton had an unofficial co-president role during Bill's tenure. Washington pundits fretted, "Who's really in charge?" That's peanuts compared to some royal courts of old where the wrong answer to that question could get you exiled or worse. For a spicier pop culture analogy: the fandom fallout from a celebrity breakup (say, the Swifties vs. whatever opposing fandom in a Taylor

Swift relationship drama) is a mild-mannered echo of the way kingdoms would divide loyalties when a king and queen were at odds. The big difference: today's fan factions fight with tweets and TikTok videos; medieval factions fought with crossbows.

In the end, the "Egos and Empire" lesson is clear – when royal spouses both crave the crown, the *marital* disputes stop being personal and start becoming political. The entire realm can become an arena for domestic discord acted out on an imperial scale. Let's be grateful that most household quarrels over who's right don't end in civil war – and let's send a nod of respect to those royal counselors of yore whose job was basically to play couples therapist to a king and queen armed with literal armies. They definitely earned their keep.

Usurpers in the Family

Most marriages vow "'til death do us part." But what happens when *one* spouse takes that as a challenge – or even a career ambition? In a few notorious royal cases, the power struggle between husband and wife got so extreme that one spouse decided they'd rather rule **alone**, marital bonds (and the other person's well-being) be damned. This is the dark, juicy side of royal matrimony: palace intrigues that escalate into coups, dethronements, and sometimes conveniently-timed funerals. Essentially, "'til death do us part" turned into a strategic plan. If this sounds like the plot of a Shakespearean tragedy or a particularly over-the-top soap opera, that's because it *is* – except it really happened. Grab the popcorn (and maybe a suit of armor) as we dive into the scandalous tales of spouses who literally usurped their partners. It's Game of Thrones: Marital Edition, and yes, occasionally someone loses a throne (or a head).

Perhaps the most famous consort-turned-coup-leader is a woman so formidable that history appended "the Great" to her name. We won't name names, but if you're guessing Catherine… you're warm. Indeed, Catherine the Great of Russia began her career as a mere royal wife – a German princess married off to the bumbling Grand Duke Peter of Russia. Catherine was intelligent, ambitious, and keenly aware that her husband (who became Tsar Peter III in 1762) was making a royal mess of things. Peter III managed to alienate just about everyone in a mere six-month reign – he offended the powerful Orthodox Church, upset the army with his weird admiration for Prussian military fashion, and in general proved as stable as a three-legged chair. Catherine, by contrast, had spent years networking, flattering the guards regiments, and positioning herself as the smarter option. So when Peter started hinting he might divorce her (and possibly send her to a convent), Catherine decided to strike first. In July 1762, she pulled off a lightning-quick coup d'état. With the help of her loyal military conspirators, Catherine rallied the St. Petersburg garrison and had herself proclaimed sole ruler of Russia. Her hapless husband Peter III was arrested and forced to abdicate that very day. Talk about a role reversal – one morning she's the unhappy wife; by evening she's the autocrat of all the Russias, crowned and everything. (Picture a modern first lady staging a coup against her president husband, getting sworn in on the same day – that's how wild this was.) The coup was so swift and smooth that Peter's reaction was reportedly one of astonishment and petulance – he *never saw it coming*. As for "'til death do us part," well… funny story: just eight days after Peter's forced abdication, he conveniently died in captivity under mysterious circumstances. Officially, it was "colic" or "apoplexy" (the 18th-century equivalent of "natural causes, we swear!"), but rumor had it Peter was *helped* to his death by one of Catherine's associates. Catherine, now Empress, shrugged off the scandal and went on to reign gloriously for decades. The episode reads like a dark comedy: a domestic squabble escalates until Wifey dearest usurps Hubby's throne and possibly has him quietly strangled – and then she becomes one of the most successful rulers in history, as if it were all just a messy divorce. Catherine's coup is proof that when one spouse says "I want to wear the crown by myself," they really mean business. She literally made death do them part – prematurely – to advance her career. Yikes.

Catherine's case might be the most famous, but it's far from the only instance of a spousal coup. For a closer-to-home (if your home is England) example, look at Isabella of France, the 14th-century Queen of England, and her husband King Edward II. Their marriage started out with the usual pomp and expectations – she was a French princess known for her beauty and savvy, he was an English king known for… well, his *very close* male favorites and less-than-stellar governing. Over time, Edward II's reign went off the rails largely because he heaped power and favor on a pair of unpopular favorites (the Despenser family), marginalizing Isabella and angering the barons. Isabella was not the demure, stand-by-your-man type. After years of being disrespected and even treated as an enemy by her husband, the Queen decided she'd had enough. While on a diplomatic trip to France, Isabella hooked up (professionally… and personally) with an exiled English lord, Roger Mortimer, who had ample reason to hate Edward. Together, Isabella and Mortimer raised an army, and in 1326 they invaded England to kick Edward II off the throne. Yes, the queen led a literal invasion against her own hubby – that's some next-level marital dispute. Edward II's support crumbled (turns out a lot of his subjects were pretty fed up with him anyway) and he was captured. Early in 1327, Isabella forced Edward to become the first English king ever to abdicate his crown. Talk about a power move: she made him hand over the kingship to their son, effectively ending his reign. Edward II later met a famously gruesome end in captivity (legend says via a red-hot poker – eesh – though historians debate that detail). In any case, Isabella got what she wanted: Edward was deposed and gone, and she ruled as regent on behalf of her young son for a few years, with Mortimer as her sidekick. Medieval chroniclers nicknamed her the "She-Wolf of France" for her ferocity, and honestly, as far as scorned spouses go, she outdid even the wildest Real Housewives revenge plot. It's the kind of story that would make a great Netflix series: a queen trades in her ineffectual husband for a newer model (ahem, Mortimer) and grabs the kingdom for herself. Move over, *House of Cards*, this is the real deal from 1327. (Claire Underwood, eat your heart out – Isabella was doing your job seven centuries earlier, in a crown no less.)

These cases illustrate the soap-operatic extreme of royal marital strife. When one spouse effectively says, "Honey, I'm overthrowing you," the marriage has *definitely* hit an all-time low. It's remarkable (and morbidly entertaining) how often the script played out: a consort feeling sidelined or endangered decides to eliminate their partner from the picture entirely. Sometimes it was outright murder; other times a forced retirement to a distant monastery or prison cell. And just like a true crime podcast, there were always whispers: Did Empress Wu Zetian of China poison her husband the Emperor to take the throne for herself? (Wu did become the only female Emperor of China, ruling in her own name – and yes, her husband died conveniently early, though she more definitively bumped off some later rivals, including her own kids. Family gatherings in the Wu household were *tense*.) Or did King Henry VIII's sixth wife Catherine Parr very nearly face a plot by her husband to execute her, only to talk her way out and outlive him – effectively "usurping" by survival since Henry died and she got to enjoy life (briefly) without that tyrant around? There's a whiff of "coup by longevity" in that one. In most cases, however, it was the women – queens and empresses – who found themselves grabbing power from husbands who underestimated them. Perhaps because queens historically had fewer formal avenues to power, some resorted to *extraordinary measures* to secure their position. It's a cautionary tale: if you don't give the spouse a meaningful role, they just might plot a palace coup. (Memo to kings: maybe let the wife chair a committee or two, just to keep her from overthrowing you.)

Modern comparisons for this are thankfully scant – we don't often see a First Lady marching into Parliament with an army. However, we can draw parallels in the corporate or political world. There have been instances in business where one spouse edged out the other from a company leadership (though usually not with literal force – shareholder votes are more the style). Or in politics, you'll occasionally see power couples where one's ambition eclipses the other: imagine if one half of a presidential couple maneuvered to take over the office *before* the term was up. (If Twitter witnessed a spouse live-tweeting a coup against a sitting president, the internet might actually break.) For a satirical example, consider the fictional Underwoods from *House of Cards* – Frank and Claire's lethal one-upmanship is basically a stylized version of what some of these royal couples did. In real life, it's more subtle: maybe a vice-president's spouse whispers advice that undermines the president, hoping their own partner will climb to power. Thankfully, outright spousal usurpation tends to be a thing of the past or the realm of fiction. It's generally frowned upon today to murder your partner for their job (HR would not approve). Still, the tales of Catherine, Isabella, and their ilk remain as thrilling reminders that in the high-stakes world of royal power, a wedding ring was sometimes the most dangerous shackle – and some spouses would do anything to break free and sit *solo* on that throne.

Two Thrones, One Household

After all these tales of strife, rebellion, and usurpation, you might be feeling a tad cynical about royal matrimony. Do any of these couples actually make it work without drawing daggers at each other? Fear not – there *were* a few shining (if rare) examples of kings and queens who found equilibrium as partners rather than rivals. Think of these as the power couples who actually balanced their power. Instead of one spouse dominating or eliminating the other, both heads managed to wear one crown – sometimes literally as co-monarchs, sometimes unofficially through mutual respect and savvy compromise. These regal duos demonstrate that with diplomacy, communication, and perhaps a good royal marriage counselor, a balance of power was possible. In this section, we profile partnerships where *mutual respect* prevailed over rivalry. Consider it a hopeful counterpoint to all the bloodier tales – proof that sometimes two heads (and two crowns) really can coexist in one household. And for a satirical modern twist, we'll sprinkle in comparisons to today's notable duos who've tried (with varying success) to share the limelight.

One of history's most successful ruling partnerships has to be Queen Isabella I of Castile and King Ferdinand II of Aragon, the Catholic Monarchs of Spain. Married in 1469, these two not only joined their kingdoms but did so with a remarkable degree of equality. Isabella was queen of the larger, richer kingdom of Castile; Ferdinand was king of Aragon. Rather than one simply subsuming the other, they figured out a kind of co-sovereignty that was highly unusual for their era. In fact, they even had a catchy motto about their teamwork: *"Tanto monta, monta tanto, Isabel como Fernando,"* which roughly means "They amount to the same, Isabella and Ferdinand." This slogan was not just for show – it reflected a real balance of power. Isabella insisted from the start that she would not be a passive queen. She famously only agreed to marry Ferdinand on the condition that he respect her authority in Castile and let her remain queen in her own right. They signed a prenuptial agreement that established equality in their partnership. (Yes, a 15th-century prenup essentially said "the power is split 50/50." Move over, Hollywood attorneys, Isabella had this idea long ago.) Throughout their reign, the two monarchs coordinated their decisions closely. They often ruled from the same court, issuing joint edicts, each one's name appearing alongside the other. Isabella focused on internal reforms and matters of Castile, Ferdinand brought his military expertise and handled a lot of the foreign policy and war strategy. They consulted each other constantly and presented a united front. One historian noted that Isabella *never* surrendered her political power to Ferdinand – she wasn't about to let "being a wife" override "being a queen". But she also valued Ferdinand's input, acknowledging his strengths especially in military affairs. The result: a dynastic duo that completed the Reconquista (the conquest of the last Moorish kingdom in Spain) together, funded Columbus's voyage together, and forged a unified Spanish monarchy as true partners. It wasn't that they never disagreed (they did, particularly over succession issues later), but they managed those disagreements without undermining each other's fundamental status. In an era when most queens were expected to defer to kings, Isabella and Ferdinand broke the mold. Their successful partnership shows that two strong-willed leaders could co-rule *if* they had a foundation of respect and a clear division of labor. We might poetically call them the original "co-CEOs" of Spain. They ran the enterprise together and rather effectively at that. The lesson in modern terms: with a solid prenup and a shared vision, even Type-A power spouses can share the corner office – or in this case, the throne room.

Another example of two royal heads being better than one comes from England's only instance (so far) of joint monarchs: William III and Mary II. Now, in fairness, *technically* their story started with a bit of a coup (they took over in the Glorious Revolution of 1688, ousting Mary's dad James II – family drama again). But what's notable is how they handled the ruling part *together* after that. Mary II was the daughter of the deposed king and had the stronger claim by blood, but her husband William of Orange was the one with the military might and political savvy that got them the crown. When Parliament offered them the throne, William made it clear he *wasn't* going to be just "Prince Consort." He would only accept if he could be king in his own right. Mary, demonstrating admirable lack of ego (or perhaps just pragmatism), supported making William co-sovereign with equal billing. So they were both crowned monarchs – a unique situation in British history. In practice, William and Mary found a workable balance: they ruled jointly, but William took lead on warfare and affairs of state when he was in England, and when he was off fighting France (which was often), Mary governed capably on her own. Far from quarreling, Mary deferred to William's judgment much of the time out of wifely respect, but when duty called, she stepped up and ran the country while he was away, to wide acclaim. It helped that they genuinely loved and respected each other – Mary once said that even if she'd been born a commoner, she'd have chosen William as her husband. (Aww.) Contemporary observers noted that Mary never let her authority as queen go to her head – she was content to let William shine, which kept his ego satisfied, and in return he trusted her and didn't object to her exercising power when necessary. They proved that *formal* co-rule could succeed, especially when each partner understood their role. Think of it as a successful job-sharing arrangement at the top of the organization chart. It's as if a company named two CEOs who actually worked well in tandem: one handles the external operations, the other keeps things running smoothly at HQ. It rarely works in business, but for

William and Mary it did – at least until Mary's untimely death from smallpox, after which William mourned her deeply (and frankly made a bit of a hash of things on his own, suggesting maybe Mary was the secret sauce all along). But for five years, England had *two* heads wearing one crown, and it wasn't a disaster – in fact it was pretty effective. Modern parallels are hard to find (there's no co-presidency to point to, though some joked that the Clintons aimed for that). However, you might liken William and Mary to a pair of co-founders of a startup who bring complementary skills and trust each other – one might be the public face while the other is the technical genius, and together they make it big. In the monarchy's case, their "startup" was the Glorious Revolution settlement, and it took both of them to stabilize the new regime.

Beyond formal arrangements, there are also royal marriages where, though only one spouse wore the crown, the other's influence was so great and so wisely managed that they effectively *co-ruled* behind the scenes. Queen Victoria and Prince Albert exemplify this. Victoria was every inch the queen regnant of the British Empire, and Albert had no official power (he wasn't even crowned, only titled Prince Consort after 17 years of marriage). But over time, Victoria came to rely deeply on Albert's counsel. Early in their marriage, she was resistant to sharing her sovereign authority – she even squabbled with him when he dared to offer political opinions, once snapping that she was the Queen and he should remember it. Albert, for his part, *hated* being a powerless ornament; he was determined to be a statesman in his own right. This could have gone badly (imagine an unhappy prince muttering in corridors, fomenting court factions). But in their case, compromise and love won out. When Victoria became overwhelmed by pregnancy and illness, she grudgingly let Albert take on some duties. He proved extremely capable – handling correspondence, advising on policy, even attending meetings with ministers. As she saw his talent and devotion, Victoria yielded more trust and authority to him. In time, Albert was *unofficially* regarded as the power behind the throne – a contemporary even called him "the uncrowned King of England". Far from resenting it, Victoria was relieved to share her burdens. The two worked as a team: Albert drove forward initiatives in education, science, industry (the Great Exhibition of 1851 was basically his project), and Victoria lent her support and royal assent. He moderated her sometimes emotional reactions and gave the monarchy a steadier, more intellectual leadership. Crucially, Albert always operated in a way that respected Victoria's ultimate role – he never undermined her publicly, and she always *formally* made the decisions he had shaped behind closed doors. This partnership dramatically strengthened the British monarchy's reputation at a time republicanism was threatening Europe's thrones. Their marriage stands as proof that a royal consort could share in ruling responsibilities without a constitutional crisis – as long as both partners communicated and respected the lines not to cross. One might say Victoria and Albert were a bit like a presidential couple where the First Lady (or First Gentleman) is a key advisor with their own policy portfolio, working in harmony with the President. (Think of the dynamic of Michelle and Barack Obama, where Michelle, while not involved in state affairs to Albert's extent, had enormous influence on social initiatives and behind-the-scenes guidance – all while making sure Barack shone in his role. In Victoria's time this was even more pronounced with Albert.) When Albert died, Victoria was devastated and Britain realized just how much of a stabilizing co-regent he had been.

We should also give a nod to other rare pairs who showed that mutual respect could eclipse power rivalry. Emperor Justinian of Byzantium and his empress Theodora were an early example (Justinian was the lawgiver and conqueror, but Theodora's counsel saved his throne during the Nika riots when he wanted to flee; she told him to stand and fight, effectively co-ruling in that crisis with nerves of steel – he listened, and by Jove, she was right). King George II of Britain and Queen Caroline of Ansbach had an interesting arrangement in the 18th century: George II wasn't exactly a feminist icon, but he *knew* his wife was the smarter of the two. He trusted Caroline so much that he appointed her regent *four times* when he went abroad to Hanover, giving her wide powers to rule in his absence. She also had great influence over him even when he was home – famously, she smoothed tensions and persuaded him on political matters, effectively moderating his decisions in concert with Sir Robert Walpole. Caroline's contemporary said that "all mankind are governed by women" and in George's case it was quite literally true (and he didn't mind). Their partnership helped ensure a stable reign and the continuity of Walpole's government, which steered Britain to prosperity. In the modern world, we see echoes of this in political couples where one spouse holds office but relies heavily on the other's expertise. Think of Franklin D. Roosevelt and Eleanor Roosevelt – FDR was president, but Eleanor was his "eyes and ears" on the ground, a policy force on civil rights and poverty, essentially a co-pilot guiding the nation's conscience. Or consider business magnates like Bill and Melinda Gates during their marriage – not royalty, but they jointly ran one of the world's largest philanthropic empires, presenting a united, co-equal front in decision-making (until their split, which, mercifully, did not involve any usurpations or prison towers).

The common thread in successful co-rule stories is communication and compromise. These couples had to park their egos at the palace door (easier said than done when you're wearing a literal crown). They had to recognize each other's strengths and let those strengths shine for the good of the realm. It's heartening, in a way, to know that even in environments that bred giant egos, some royals managed to make marriage a partnership of equals – or as close to equals as possible given the era. They leave us not just colorful stories, but also some *lessons* in diplomacy for any power-sharing relationship. Lesson one: respect and trust are mightier than decrees and titles. Lesson two: play to each other's strengths (if your queen is a better diplomat, maybe let her handle French ambassadors while you handle the battlefield, or vice versa). Lesson three: keep the lines of communication open – a secret to these partnerships was that the king and queen actually *talked* and listened to one another in private council. And perhaps lesson four: a little humility goes a long way; even a king can admit his wife has a point (looking at you, Justinian, thanking Theodora for that don't-flee pep talk that saved your reign).

In our age, the idea of two people jointly holding ultimate power is rare, but we do cherish the notion of the "power couple" – two individuals who are each accomplished and influential in their own right, choosing to walk side by side. When it works, it's like watching a great duet: each one enhances the other. For a satirical contrast, imagine if some of our modern high-profile pairs tried to literally share a throne. Prince Harry and Meghan Markle – well, they kind of did the opposite, stepping *away* from the throne's orbit to find balance. Jay-Z and Beyoncé – they rule the music world together; one day Beyoncé might jokingly say she's the only Queen in that house, but you know Jay respects her sway. We've also seen political tag-teams like Nelson Mandela and Winnie Mandela (in their early years) or Justin Trudeau and his wife Sophie Gregoire Trudeau (who, while not a co-ruler, used her platform for advocacy, complementing his public image – at least until their recent separation, proving even modern fairy tales can end). The truth is, any marriage of strong individuals is a balancing act, and royal marriages are just that with more pomp and pressure. The happy co-rule stories remind us it *can* be done.

So there we have it: from domestic duels to dynamic duos. Royal history runs the gamut of marital experiences more dramatically than any Netflix series. We've seen the humorous squabbles over "who gets to be boss tonight," the frightening battles of wills that spilled into open conflict, the Machiavellian plots where one spouse simply removes the other from the equation, and the enlightened partnerships where two rulers learned to share the throne (or at least the decision-making). Fun Facts, Throne for Two isn't just a cheeky title – as we've learned, a throne built for two can sometimes foster cooperation… or spark a battle royal. The secret lives of kings and queens, when the cameras stop rolling, turn out to be strikingly similar to any marriage – just magnified by power and privilege. In the end, whether you're a royal or a commoner, marriage might just boil down to figuring out who takes out the trash, who takes out the traitorous advisor, and who takes the lead when ruling an empire – all before bedtime. And if you can manage that with humor and love, you've already won the only war that really matters.

Chapter 5

Scandals and Side Pieces – The Royal Art of Infidelity

Welcome back to our royal circus, where crowns are shiny, but fidelity? Not so much. In this chapter, we're pulling back the velvet curtain on one of monarchy's worst-kept secrets: kings and queens behaving *badly*. Think of it as a behind-the-scenes tour of palace boudoirs and broom closets, all delivered with a wink. From "official" mistresses who got their own palace apartments to queens plotting poison in the wine goblet, history proves that when it came to marriage, many royals treated vows like a suggestion rather than a rule. By the end of this romp, you'll see that a king's extramarital antics were often an open secret – practically a job perk – while a queen daring to do the same was playing with literal fire. Infidelity in royal courts came with *gasp*-worthy double standards, high-stakes drama, and occasional international fallout. So fluff up the throne cushions and prepare for some juicy tales of regal two-timing, told in our signature quirky, charming tone. Let's spill the tea (poison-free, we promise) on the *royal art of infidelity*.

The Open Secret: Mistress Culture

In many monarchies, monogamy was about as real as a unicorn grazing in the palace garden. For kings, having a mistress (or three) was less scandal and more *standard operating procedure*. Welcome to the world of the royal mistress, a semi-institutionalized role that was the worst-kept secret in court. Everyone knew the score: the queen provided the heirs and decorum, while the mistress provided... let's say "supplemental services" and excitement on the side. The arrangement was so common that some royal courts openly accommodated mistresses – sometimes even giving these "unofficial" lovers very *official* perks like titles, staff, spending allowances, and plush apartments within the palace walls. In 17th-century France, for example, the king's chief mistress held the title *maîtresse-en-titre* (literally "official mistress") and could live in style just a few doors down from the queen. Awkward? Oh, absolutely. But for the courtiers and staff, it was just another Tuesday when the monarch's favorite lady (who wasn't his wife) strolled by with a confident smile.

The craziest part is that this "mistress culture" wasn't even considered particularly scandalous *by royal standards*. It was practically expected. Remember, for much of history, royal marriages were arranged for political gain, not passion. The king and queen might exchange vows at the altar, but behind closed doors, the king often had a roster of "special friends" to keep him company. These mistresses weren't sneaking in via secret tunnels (well, not always) – they often had a semi-recognized place at court. In some cases, they wielded genuine influence, acting as the proverbial "power behind the throne". They could whisper political advice in the monarch's ear between pillow talks, or introduce artists and philosophers to the king (Madame de Pompadour, chief mistress of Louis XV, practically ran France's cultural scene, acting like an unofficial minister of arts).

Indeed, history's most infamous side pieces often became celebrities in their own right. These weren't downtrodden secret lovers; many were celebrated courtesans or high-born ladies who became political players by virtue of the king's favor. They could make or break careers at court with a well-placed word. One royal mistress in England, Alice Perrers (lover of King Edward III), was showered with so many gifts and perks that folks wondered if she'd *bewitched* the king. (Public opinion of her was less than kind – one chronicler called her "that unspeakable whore who always satisfied all his desires of the flesh" – not exactly a subtle job description.) In France, the official mistresses like Madame de Montespan or Madame de Pompadour were essentially *institutions.* They dined with dukes, interceded for petitioners, and patronized great artists. These women had *swagger.* They weren't just arm candy; they dished out favors, influenced policy, and sometimes even convinced the king who to ally with or who gets to head the treasury. Think of them as a combination of chief of staff, cultural minister, and BFF – with benefits – to the king.

Meanwhile, what about the poor queen in this scenario? Often, the queen had to endure this arrangement with a tight, formal smile and a stiff upper lip (perhaps grinding her teeth when no one was looking). Many a royal wife found ways to cope. Some took up hobbies – charity work, fashion, even flirtation at court (within safe limits, because heaven forbid the queen actually have *her* own side piece – we'll get to that double standard soon). Others formed polite friendships with the mistresses, bizarre as that sounds. In one case, King Charles II of England's wife, Queen Catherine, was said to have tolerated his many mistresses, even as those women like Nell Gwyn and Barbara Castlemaine lived nearby in Whitehall Palace. You can imagine the palace breakfast scene: the queen at one end of the table buttering her toast with dignity, while the king's favorite from last night might saunter in late, accepting a cup of tea from a servant – tension you could cut with a knife. But in the convoluted etiquette of royal courts, everyone pretended this was fine. After all, for the monarch, infidelity was practically a status symbol – a perk of power and virility.

This open secret of mistress culture wasn't confined to one country or era, either. Globally, royals had their "side arrangements." Chinese emperors had harems of consorts; Ottoman sultans had whole harems too, though those were polygamous setups with legal status for multiple wives. European kings, stuck (in theory) with one wife due to Christian monogamy rules, simply bent the rules by keeping mistresses. From France's palace of Versailles to the courts of India's Maharajas, powerful men indulged in multiple lovers with a nudge-nudge wink from their advisors. The difference was in branding: in Europe they were "ladies-in-waiting" or *maîtresses déclarées*, in other places they might be courtesans or concubines. The outcome was the same – monogamy took a backseat to monarchy.

Let's spill some specific historical tea. Take France's King Louis XIV – the *Sun King* himself. He didn't just have one mistress; he had an official chief mistress and then a lineup of lesser flings. His maîtresse-en-titre had her own wing in Versailles, for heaven's sake. Louis's most famous mistress, Madame de Montespan, bore him multiple children and reigned as unofficial queen of his heart for years. She even got jealous when younger women caught the king's eye, like a star quarterback's girlfriend guarding her turf. (In fact, Montespan's jealousy turned lethal – but hold that thought for our "Dangerous Liaisons" section, where poison makes an appearance.) Across the channel, King Charles II of England wasn't far behind in the mistress department. He installed his principal mistress, Barbara Palmer (Lady Castlemaine), in a palace suite directly above his wife's chambers. Yes, you read that right – the mistress literally upstairs from the queen. It was said you could trace Charles's morning routine by the creaking of the floorboards from Barbara's bedroom down to Catherine's breakfast room. Awkward with a capital A.

The *official mistress* role, as twisted as it sounds now, had a weird semi-respectability. Courtiers would curry favor with the king *through* his mistress: "Madame, could you mention to His Majesty the matter of my estate?" Flattery, gifts, bribes – all went to the mistress in hopes she'd whisper support to the king. Some mistresses effectively acted as gatekeepers. They even had staff and ladies-in-waiting of their own. A few were granted noble titles in their own right (King Louis XV made his top mistress, Madame de Pompadour, the Marquise de Pompadour – she wasn't born a noble, he just went *ta-da!* and gave her a title). When you have a situation where the king's girlfriend is granting political favors while the queen is busy christening ships and opening hospitals, you know monogamy has left the building.

And lest we think it was only the men having fun – occasionally, a reigning queen or empress had her paramours too (though far more discreetly). For instance, Empress Catherine the Great of Russia kept a stable of handsome "favorites" once she was widowed and wielding power in her own right – essentially the reverse of mistress culture. She bestowed titles and gifts on her lovers, setting them up nicely (ah, equality at last, sort of). But cases like Catherine were rare and required that the woman be the sovereign ruler; a queen consort married to a king usually did *not* have such liberty. Generally, the open secret of extramarital romance was a one-way street favoring the king. As we're about to see, that double standard was enormous – big enough to park a royal carriage in.

Double Standards, Double Beds

If extramarital affairs in royal marriages were practically the rule for kings, they were absolutely forbidden fruit for queens. Welcome to the hilariously lopsided moral landscape of royal fidelity. It's a tale as old as monarchy: the king winks at his own dalliances as a harmless perk of power, while the queen even *glancing* at a handsome courtier could land her in exile, a convent, or six feet under. The double standard wasn't just gossip – it was codified in culture and sometimes even law. Kings got a pat on the back for virility; queens got the axe (sometimes literally) for *any* hint of infidelity. Comedy and tragedy lived side by side in this royal hypocrisy.

Let's illustrate with a jaw-dropping example. One medieval king – we won't name names (okay, fine, it was Henry I of England) – managed to father at least twenty-two illegitimate children with a parade of mistresses. Twenty-two! He practically had enough extra kids to start his own football league. Did this prolific cheating damage his reputation? Not really. King Henry I openly acknowledged many of these offspring, gave his sons titles, married his daughters off to nobles – the whole kingdom knew about his bustling sideline in baby-making. Far from hiding it, he treated it as proof that *hey, the king's still got it*. In that era, people almost expected a king to have a few "bastards" – it was seen as a sign of virility and even a backup plan for the dynasty (more royal spawn, even if unofficial). Meanwhile, Henry's queen (and subsequent wives of other kings) were lauded as "good wives" for politely looking the other way.

This pattern repeats across history. A king might boast in private that he was a *good husband* because, say, he didn't divorce his wife despite her failing to produce an heir – all while he sired a small army of kids with mistresses. The mental gymnastics here are worthy of an Olympic gold. For example, a certain European monarch (picture a smug king with a chestful of medals) was rumored to congratulate himself for not casting off his "barren" wife, even as he racked up illegitimate progeny well into the double digits. In his mind, staying married to his queen – who suffered the heartbreak of infertility – made him saintly, never mind the string of mistress-fueled nurseries he kept stocked. If that doesn't make you shake your head and laugh, what will?

Now flip the script: imagine a queen or princess doing even a fraction of that. Oh, the outrage! Royal women were expected to exhibit unyielding chastity and loyalty, even if their husbands gallivanted about. The reason for this sexist double standard was partly political: a king's extramarital kids were usually not in line for the throne (they were deemed "bastards" legally and thus cut out of succession). So while embarrassing, the king's philandering didn't threaten the royal lineage. A queen's affair, however, could call into question the paternity of a future heir – a big no-no. Queenly adultery was seen as undermining the legitimacy of the entire dynasty, striking at the very heart of monarchy. That's why when a queen *was* even suspected of cheating, the reaction made the Spanish Inquisition look mild.

History provides plentiful examples of this absurd asymmetry. One of the most tragic is Anne Boleyn, the second wife of England's King Henry VIII. When Henry VIII got tired of Anne (ironic, since he moved heaven and earth – and split from the Catholic Church – to marry her in the first place), he accused her of adultery. Whether Anne actually cheated is highly doubtful (most historians say those charges were trumped up), but it didn't matter – the mere *idea* of a queen's infidelity was so unacceptable that Anne lost her crown and then her head. Literally. A French swordsman was imported for the occasion of her execution, because royal adultery was apparently a crime deserving special effects. Another of Henry VIII's wives, Catherine Howard, *did* have a fling with a handsome courtier. Result: the young queen met the same fate as Anne. Two queens executed for infidelity (or rumors of it), while King Henry himself had been serially unfaithful to each of his wives without consequence. Double standard, much?

Even when the outcome wasn't as bloody, adulterous queens or princesses were harshly punished. In 14th-century France, a scandal known as the Nesle Tower affair blew up when King Philip IV's daughters-in-law were caught in extramarital affairs. Two princesses had allegedly been rendezvousing with knights in a secluded tower in Paris – basically a medieval *love nest*. When this came to light, all hell broke loose. The princesses were arrested and locked away; their lovers were tortured and brutally executed (reports say the unlucky knights were even flayed alive, which gives new meaning to "getting skinned" for cheating). One of the princesses died in prison, possibly murdered to hush things up. The kicker? This scandal didn't just ruin a few lives – it sparked a succession crisis. With those princesses disgraced, their marriages to the king's sons collapsed, and within a generation, the direct royal line went extinct, helping ignite the Hundred Years' War between France and England. Talk about consequences. A couple of extramarital flings literally triggered decades of warfare. Meanwhile, kings of that era carried on with mistresses rather openly and nobody started a war over *that*.

The lopsided morality didn't go unnoticed by contemporaries either – some commented on the absurdity of it, albeit quietly. A king's affair might be gossiped about over dinner, sometimes even joked about in cheeky poems or satires, but it rarely threatened his reign. On the other hand, a queen merely appearing *too friendly* with a man not her husband could become a political crisis. Consider the case of Queen Caroline of Brunswick in the 19th century. She was the estranged wife of Britain's King George IV. George was openly adulterous (he had multiple mistresses and a secret wife before Caroline, a whole mess of infidelity on his part), but when Caroline was rumored to have taken an Italian lover during their separation, George moved to have her stripped of her title. He dragged her name through the mud in an adultery trial in

Parliament – a huge scandal that captivated the public. The people actually sided with Caroline, seeing the double standard clearly: why punish the queen for a dalliance when the king had been unfaithful from day one? Mobs shouted in her support, pamphlets lambasted the king's hypocrisy, and Caroline became a folk hero of sorts for standing up to the double standard. It was like a twisted early 1800s reality show: "Royal Marriage Scandal: *She* might have cheated – *he* definitely did – tune in for the public spectacle!"

All these examples drive home the same point: for royal men, extramarital affairs were tacitly accepted, even expected. Kings often prided themselves on their virility – having mistresses and bonus children was practically part of the job description (the *unwritten* part). For royal women, any hint of infidelity was catastrophic. They were expected to be paragons of virtue, silently bearing their husbands' indiscretions with a demure curtsey and a forced smile. It's the kind of hypocrisy that's so outrageous, you have to laugh – and also maybe cry a little, out of sympathy for those poor queens. The comedy is in how oblivious these kings could be (patting themselves on the back for *not divorcing* the wife they were betraying nightly), and the tragedy is in how many women suffered under this double standard. As one historian quipped, a king's bastards were no threat to the crown, but a queen's lover could topple the kingdom. So the next time you hear someone nostalgically praising "the good old days of chivalry and honor," remind them that those days involved some royally ridiculous double standards in the bedroom department.

Jealous Queens and Dangerous Liaisons

Hell hath no fury like a woman scorned – especially if that woman wears a crown. Being the wronged party in a royal love triangle could drive even the most prim and proper queen to *creative extremes*. After all, if you're a queen who's been publicly humiliated by the king's mistress, you have a few options: grin and bear it, retreat to your chateau and focus on your embroidery, or plot elaborate revenge on your rival. Care to guess which option some queens chose? You got it – welcome to the *Real Housewives of the Palace* drama edition, featuring jealous queens, scheming mistresses, and the occasional dash of murder. And it wasn't just queens; sometimes kings themselves got entangled in dangerous liaisons, where a lover's quarrel could escalate into a full-blown political crisis or even war. Who knew pillow talk could be so perilous?

First, let's talk about queens dealing with mistresses. Some royal wives swallowed their pride; others decided to *eliminate* the competition – literally. There are spicy court rumors and anecdotes of queens who tried to poison their husband's lovers. One notorious episode from 17th-century France is the Affair of the Poisons, a scandal that unmasked a web of nobles dabbling in black magic and poison. Caught up in this was King Louis XIV's chief mistress, Madame de Montespan. So powerful was Montespan's hold over the king that when younger women caught his eye, she allegedly resorted to hiring fortune-tellers and *poisoners* to take out the competition. Yes, the king's mistress was poisoning *other* mistresses – you know the situation is bonkers when the side pieces are trying to off each other. But rumor had it even the queen, Maria Theresa, got involved indirectly: fed up with her husband's flagrant affair, the pious queen prayed for divine intervention while Montespan stirred literal witch's brews to keep the king's love. In this high-stakes soap opera, one mistress was said to have been poisoned at a royal dinner, and suspicious deaths of several young ladies at court were whispered to be Montespan's handiwork. The king eventually dismissed Montespan once the poisoning scandal broke (nothing like a little murder plot to kill the romance). Though Louis XIV brushed it under the rug, the message was clear – jealousy in the royal bedroom could be *deadly*.

Then there's the legendary showdown of Queen vs. Mistress in Renaissance France: Catherine de' Medici versus Diane de Poitiers. Catherine was the long-suffering wife of King Henry II. Diane de Poitiers was Henry's older, glamorous mistress who basically had him wrapped around her finger for decades. Catherine played nice while Henry lived, but the second he died (jousting accident, ironically while wearing Diane's favor in the tournament), Catherine wasted no time. She promptly evicted Diane from her luxurious palace apartments and *confiscated her jewels*. According to some accounts, Catherine even took back a prized château (Chenonceau) that Henry had given Diane, forcing Diane to swap it for a lesser château. That's the polite, royal version of revenge – legalistic and property-based. Unconfirmed gossip claimed Catherine might have also slipped Diane a little slow-acting poison as a parting gift (there's speculation that Diane's later ill health was due to gold poisoning from a potion – possibly a bit of Catherine's *Italian* hospitality). While hard evidence of poison is lacking, one thing is certain: Catherine spent years stewing in jealousy and, once in power, she neutralized her rival with brutal efficiency (no heads rolled, but reputations and fortunes surely did).

Not all jealous reactions were so behind-the-scenes. Sometimes, they caused international scandals. Let's revisit that earlier mention of Britain's King George I and his unfortunate wife, Sophia Dorothea. George, back when he was a Hanoverian prince, wasn't exactly a loving husband – he kept a mistress openly and ignored Sophia. Lonely and neglected, Sophia Dorothea fell into an affair with a dashing Swedish count named Königsmarck. When George found out, it did not end well (understatement alert). The count mysteriously disappeared – rumor says George had him killed and his body disposed of under the palace floorboards. As for Sophia Dorothea, she was divorced in all but name and locked away in a castle for the rest of her life, forbidden from seeing her children. Fast forward a few years, George becomes King of Great Britain, and he still refuses to acknowledge or free his imprisoned ex. This turned into a bit of a diplomatic embarrassment – a German princess locked up indefinitely – but as king, George simply didn't care. Thus, a royal love triangle ended with a murder (most likely) and a princess in permanent time-out. It's like a grim fairy tale: *The King, the Queen, and the Mistress in the Iron Mask.* Jealousy can escalate, indeed.

Sometimes, the lover's drama spilled beyond palace walls into geopolitics. One particularly dramatic case: Henry VIII of England, who is basically the poster child for letting love life chaos reshape history. His dangerous liaison with Anne Boleyn (while married to Catherine of Aragon) didn't lead to murder out of jealousy by a queen – instead, it led

Henry himself to break with the Catholic Church when the Pope wouldn't grant him a quick divorce. The result? The English Reformation. England turned Protestant largely because the king's affair (and obsession to wed Anne) couldn't be legitimized under Catholic law. So there you have it — a royal affair that sparked religious upheaval and international tensions for generations. When Anne Boleyn failed to produce a son and allegedly flirted with others, Henry's affections curdled into the aforementioned execution. That lover's quarrel (well, one-sided quarrel, poor Anne) sent shockwaves through Europe.

We also have instances where a monarch's extramarital entanglements triggered outright conflict. Consider the saga of Paris, Helen, and Menelaus — yes, going all the way back to ancient myth/history here. The Trojan War (if you believe Homer) kicked off because a Trojan prince (Paris) ran off with a Greek king's wife (Helen). One illicit romance, and next thing you know, a thousand ships are launched, Troy is burning, and Brad Pitt is starring in a movie about it millennia later. That's perhaps the OG example of a "dangerous liaison" that reshaped history through war. Closer to factual history, recall the French Nesle affair we discussed: that scandal of adulterous princesses didn't just end with personal tragedy; it altered the succession in France and gave the English crown an opening to claim the French throne, fueling the Hundred Years' War. Who would guess that a few secret trysts in a tower could help plunge nations into conflict? Truth really is stranger than fiction.

And let's not forget those "secret love children" who occasionally showed up and rattled the monarchy. Infidelities often produced offspring, and if the wrong person acknowledged them, it could spell trouble. One juicy case: King Charles II of England had a mistress, Lucy Walter, who bore a son. Rumors swirled that Charles had actually married Lucy in secret, which, if true, would make her boy the legitimate heir. This was never proven (and is likely false), but that secret love child – James, Duke of Monmouth – grew up thinking he might claim the throne. After Charles II died, Monmouth indeed declared himself the rightful king and even led a rebellion. All because his mom was the king's side piece and gossip hinted he was "official." The rebellion failed (heads rolled, as they do), but it's a classic example of how a royal affair, if not discreet, could spiral into armed insurrection. When monarchs played loose with marital fidelity, the fallout sometimes went beyond just gossip – it threatened the stability of realms.

So, we've seen poisonings, imprisonments, wars, and rebellions – all stemming from infidelity and jealousy under crown. It's the stuff of melodrama, except it actually happened. Queens often had little recourse against philandering husbands, but the truly formidable ones found ways to *get even*, or at least make their displeasure known. And kings, for their part, sometimes let passion (or lust) drive them to reckless decisions that statesmen would later have to clean up. You could say royal infidelity had a body count and a price tag. But beyond the sensationalism, these dangerous liaisons also humanized the players. A cuckolded queen plotting revenge? A king risking it all for love or lust? Stripped of their crowns, these are very human reactions – jealousy, heartache, desire. It just so happens that when royals had them, the stakes were a tad higher than for us common folk. In a way, these episodes show that kings and queens, for all their divine-right posturing, were ultimately governed by the same emotions as anybody else – they just had the means to indulge or avenge them on a grand scale.

Affairs to Remember (an`d Regret)

What happens when a royal affair stops being discreet and becomes front-page news (or front-pamphlet news, in olden times)? In other words, what about the scandals that *didn't* stay secret? From medieval gossip broadsheets to modern paparazzi lenses, the public exposure of blue-blooded misbehavior has always been explosive – equal parts schadenfreude and shock for the masses. In this section, we'll recount some famous "caught-in-the-act" moments and their fallout. We'll see reputations ruined, marriages strained to the breaking point, and the occasional forced abdication or exile. Yet, paradoxically, these very scandals often ended up humanizing monarchs in the public eye. Nothing says "Hey, they're just like us!" quite like a king getting busted sneaking out of someone else's bedroom or a queen caught in a compromising letter exchange. It's comforting, in a twisted way, for us peasants to know that even the high and mighty end up in the doghouse.

Let's start in the days before mass media, when word-of-mouth and the printing press had to do the job of TMZ and Twitter. Even centuries ago, there was an appetite for royal scandal. In 16th- and 17th-century Europe, if a king's affair became too obvious, you might find cheeky poems or satirical woodcut pamphlets circulating in marketplaces. These were the medieval scandal sheets, often anonymous, that dished dirt on monarchs with amusing (or obscene) illustrations. For example, during the French Revolution, underground pamphleteers published lewd cartoons and stories about Queen Marie Antoinette's supposed orgies and lovers – pure fabrication, but widely believed and hugely damaging to her reputation. Earlier, in the 18th century, French pamphlets took aim at King Louis XV and his mistresses, depicting the king as a debauched libertine. One might see a crude woodcut of the king sneaking a young courtesan into a bedroom window while the queen prays alone. These pamphlets were the tabloids of their day, and royals feared them. It's one thing to have a mistress; it's another for all of Paris or London to be giggling about it. Public exposure was the great equalizer – it turned the private misdeeds of a monarch into common gossip, tarnishing the magic of the crown.

Sometimes, the public got *actual* evidence of a tryst – a caught-in-the-act moment. Consider the case of King Charles II's successor, King James II of England. He had a very public affair with his mistress Catherine Sedley. James showered Sedley with titles and money, and their relationship was so blatant that it scandalized even the loose-moraled Restoration court. Pamphlets lambasted James for keeping a mistress *while* trying to promote his image as a devout Catholic king. People started to say James's moral lapses reflected on his ability to rule. It was one ingredient in the sour mix that led to his ouster in the Glorious Revolution. In short, a king's public infidelity can speed up his downfall if the political winds are already against him.

Jumping ahead to the 19th century: technology arrived to make royal scandal even more public. The invention of newspapers (with wide circulation) and later photography meant royals had nowhere to hide. One royal who learned this the hard way was King Edward VII of Britain (before he was king, known as Prince Albert Edward, or "Bertie"). Bertie was a playboy prince, and one of his youthful dalliances actually made the papers in a big way. In 1870, a scandal known as the Mordaunt divorce case hit the courts. A noblewoman sued her husband for divorce, naming Prince Bertie as one of her lovers. Suddenly, the future king of England was dragged into court as a witness, and the whole empire gawked at newspaper reports of the Prince in a witness box, admitting to *visiting* this married lady (nudge nudge). The public was titillated and appalled. Queen Victoria (Bertie's mother) was mortified at her son's embarrassment. Bertie managed to survive it – he wasn't the one on trial, after all – but his reputation took a hit as a philanderer. This was an affair gone public in the Victorian age, and it proved that even tightly-controlled royal images could be cracked by scandal.

For a truly nuclear example of public exposure, look at the saga of King Edward VIII in 1936. This is the famous case of a king who *didn't* keep his affair discreet – and it cost him the throne. Edward VIII fell deeply in love with Wallis Simpson, an American divorcee. Dating her openly as king was bad enough, but when he decided he wanted to marry her, that set off a constitutional crisis. For a while, the British press (under pressure) kept silent about the affair even though foreign papers ran it – a last gasp of media deference. But by December 1936, the story exploded in Britain. Headlines blared that the King was intent on marrying "that woman." The public was scandalized that their unmarried king was romantically entangled with a twice-divorced American (this was *very* not okay by the conservative standards of the time). The Church opposed it, the government threatened to resign – it was chaos. In the end, Edward VIII abdicated – gave up his crown "for the woman I love," as he famously said on radio. Talk about fallout: a sitting monarch lost his job because his private life became public and unacceptable. Some folks found it romantic ("aww, he sacrificed his throne for love!"), but many in Britain were outraged at the mess it caused. In a weird twist, though, Edward's very public abdication actually *saved* the monarchy's reputation long-term: his stolid younger brother (George VI) took over and steered the crown back to respectability. Still, the Edward/Wallis affair remains one of history's most dramatic examples of an indiscretion becoming international front-page news.

Modern times have only amplified this phenomenon. Today's royals face 24/7 media and the omnipresent smartphone camera. There's practically no room for the kind of "contained" mistress arrangements of old. If a prince sneezes in the wrong company, someone's tweeting about it. We've seen royal infidelity scandals play out in real time: paparazzi snapping photos of illicit rendezvous, leaked phone recordings of not-so-proper conversations (looking at you, 1990s "Camillagate" tape of Prince Charles sweet-talking Camilla – the less said about his tampon comment, the better). The world cringed and laughed simultaneously, but also perhaps thought, "Well, even a future king can make a fool of himself in love." In another instance, tabloids splashed pictures of a topless Duchess of York (Sarah Ferguson) getting her toes sucked by a boyfriend by a pool – a humiliation that led to her essentially being ousted from the royal family's inner circle. When Princess Diana famously said "there were three of us in this marriage" referring to Charles's longtime affair, the public sympathy overwhelmingly went to Diana, and the Prince of Wales got a drubbing in the court of public opinion. These contemporary examples mirror the age-old pattern: once a royal affair hits the public eye, it *will* cause turmoil.

The fallout from exposure can range from merely embarrassing to utterly catastrophic. In some cases, marriages are strained to the breaking point or end in divorce. In others, careers are derailed – a royal might lose military ranks or public esteem. Occasionally, someone has to literally quit being royal (Edward VIII's abdication being the prime case). But there's also that ironic silver lining: these scandals can humanize royals. Seeing a king caught in a love trap of his own making can oddly endear him to people – "See, he's not a lofty demi-god, he's just a guy who got in trouble with his wife." Historically, subjects often enjoyed seeing a bit of comeuppance for haughty monarchs. The gossip rags selling fast indicated a certain glee in imagining the king sleeping on the proverbial couch. In a way, when royals stumble in love, they lose some mystique but gain relatability.

Take the example of a very recent royal imbroglio: King Juan Carlos I of Spain. In 2012, it was revealed (via a bizarre incident where he broke his hip on a secret safari trip) that the king had been off in Botswana with a woman who was not his queen. The news erupted – Spaniards were livid not just about the affair but that he was elephant-hunting on a lavish trip during an economic recession. The double whammy of scandal forced Juan Carlos to apologize publicly and ultimately contributed to his abdication a couple years later. Here's a king taken down a peg, made to appear as a flawed old man who made poor choices. While embarrassing for the monarchy, it also served as a reminder: even kings are accountable nowadays, at least to public opinion.

In summary, the public exposure of royal affairs has always been a sensational affair in itself. Whether via gossip pamphlet or telephoto lens, such revelations strip away the aura of infallibility from monarchs. Some handle it with grace and humor – others not so much. Marriages may crumble, and sometimes crowns are lost. Yet these very scandals have a curious democratizing effect: they turn kings and queens into soap opera protagonists in the eyes of their subjects. It's hard to hold someone up as God's anointed ruler when you've seen their dirty laundry (sometimes literally) aired out. On the bright side, scandal also means that when a king apologizes to his queen or a prince mends his ways, people nod and say, "Been there, done that." It's relatable. After all, who hasn't experienced or witnessed some romantic misstep or domestic squabble? Of course, for us it doesn't usually make global headlines – but we can empathize.

So, as we close this chapter on royal infidelity, what have we learned? Kings and queens, despite all their pomp and privilege, are not immune to temptation, jealousy, folly, and passion. In fact, they often indulged in these more than the average person *because* they could – and because the stakes (heirs, alliances, egos) were so high. Mistresses became institutions, double standards ran rampant, jealous showdowns occasionally turned lethal, and public scandals shook thrones. It's a rich tapestry of human drama, played out on the grandest stage. And through it all, one can't help but chuckle at the absurdity: the people who had everything – crowns, castles, absolute power – still struggled to keep their love lives in check. Maybe that's the ultimate lesson and the big, cosmic joke. Royal or not, when it comes to affairs of the heart (and the loins), we're all only human. Even a king can get sent to the doghouse – and yes, sometimes even a king has to sleep on the couch (or in his case, a very ornate chaise longue) when the cameras stop rolling and the chickens come home to roost.

In the next chapter, we'll continue our irreverent tour behind palace doors – but for now, keep these fun (and cautionary) facts in mind. Monogamy in monarchy often *was* as real as a unicorn, but the fallout of infidelity was very real indeed. The throne may seat two, but as we've seen, there were often more people in the royal bedchamber than officially advertised. And that, dear reader, is both the secret and the scandal of how royal couples really live when the cameras stop rolling.

Chapter 6

Heirs, Spares, and Royal Parenting Nightmares

Welcome to the royal nursery, where pacifiers and politics collide. In this chapter, we peek behind the gilded curtains at how kings and queens handled (or fumbled) the whole "having kids" thing – from the pressure to pop out a male heir on demand, to the inevitable sibling squabbles over who gets the big chair, to the absolutely bizarre parenting practices that make your family's quirks look quaint. It's a humorous journey through the age-old saga of Heirs, Spares, and Royal Parenting Nightmares, proving that when it comes to raising little princes and princesses, even the most blue-blooded parents often found themselves royally in over their heads.

The Heir Apparent Pressure Cooker

In royal marriages, romance often took a backseat to reproduction – specifically, the production of an heir apparent. The prime directive was simple in theory (if nerve-wracking in practice): *have a baby boy*. The stability of the dynasty, the continuation of the bloodline, and the peace of the realm depended on it. No heir meant *succession crisis*, which in those days was practically an invitation to civil war among ambitious relatives. (History offers plenty of examples – from medieval wars of succession to the War of the Spanish Succession – where a monarch's death without a clear heir led to chaos and conflict.) So, you can imagine the mood in the royal bedroom wasn't exactly candlelight and roses; it was more like a high-stakes fertility exam with an entire kingdom pacing in the waiting room.

For queens especially, being *"fertile"* was the top job requirement – fertile above all else, personality optional. These women were expected to be basically heir-producing machines, a term no doubt coined by a court cynic after one too many awkward baby christenings. If a queen consort failed to produce a son in a timely manner, she risked *enormous* backlash – from public disappointment and court gossip to, in extreme cases, humiliation, annulment, or worse. As unchivalrous as it sounds, many kings treated their wives' wombs as national security assets. A successful delivery of a healthy boy could earn a queen praise and love; repeated deliveries of daughters or miscarriages could earn her side-eye glances and prayers for improvement. (Never mind that no one in the Renaissance had a clue about the science of baby-making – we now know it's the father's sperm that actually determines a baby's sex, but back then, if it wasn't a boy, it was automatically the queen's fault. Talk about a royal injustice!)

Perhaps no monarch better illustrates the *heir-or-bust* mentality than England's King Henry VIII. This guy turned the heir pressure up to 11 and then broke the knob. Henry was *obsessed* with securing a male successor and went to extreme lengths to achieve it. When his first wife, the admirable Catherine of Aragon, bore him only a daughter (the future Mary I) and had multiple miscarriages and stillbirths in her desperate attempts to give him a son, Henry's patience (never his strong suit) ran out. Deciding that *clearly* the marriage was cursed (or that a newer model wife might do the trick), Henry asked the Pope for an annulment. The Pope, wary of upsetting Catherine's powerful relatives, refused. So Henry – egotistical and determined – essentially said, "Fine, I'll do it myself." In a move that redefined *extra*, he broke with the Roman Catholic Church entirely and declared himself head of a new Church of England just so he could dump Catherine and marry someone else. Yes, the man changed his kingdom's whole religion because the marriage hadn't produced a boy – talk about a dramatic breakup. (If you thought ghosting was bad, try founding a new church to avoid your ex!).

Henry's saga didn't end there. He married *again* to the youthful Anne Boleyn, hoping she'd be the one to give him the coveted son. Anne did give birth – but to a girl (the future Elizabeth I). That was not the result Henry wanted on the scoreboard. After a series of miscarriages and no prince, Henry grew convinced that Anne too had failed the "heir exam." His solution was as subtle as a beheading. In 1536, he had Anne executed on trumped-up charges (treason, adultery, witchcraft – you name it) and promptly married Wife #3. To Henry's relief, the third time was the charm: Jane Seymour bore him Prince Edward, a bona fide male heir. Henry was so overjoyed that he likely did a little Tudor jig in his jewel-encrusted codpiece. (Poor Jane Seymour died soon after childbirth, but Henry would forever call her his *"true"* wife for providing his longed-for son.) This king's heir obsession was literally a life-or-death matter for his wives. He ultimately went through six wives in his quest for a stable line of succession – two divorced, two beheaded, one died, one survived (lucky her). As one summary puts it, Henry was "egotistical, paranoid and desperate for a male heir," willing to marry six times and even kill friends and wives who couldn't give him what he wanted. All in the name of securing that bouncing baby boy on the throne.

Henry VIII's story may be the most infamous, but he wasn't the only ruler who treated "siring an heir" as the be-all and end-all of marriage. Across Europe and beyond, many a royal couple felt the heat of the heir-hunting spotlight. In fact, the pressure was universal in monarchies: if no male heir arrived, the dynasty's future hung in the balance. For example, the Tudor dynasty Henry was so anxious to continue had itself come to power amid a succession crisis (the Wars of the Roses) decades earlier – something Henry was terrified of repeating. Over in France, the stakes were just as high. Fast forward a couple centuries: Napoleon Bonaparte, the French Emperor, actually divorced his beloved first wife Joséphine mainly because she hadn't given him a son. He adored Josephine, but eventually *realpolitik* and baby fever took over – "Sorry, my love, it's not you, it's your womb." In 1810 he annulled the marriage and promptly married Marie-Louise of Austria, a teenage princess chosen for her healthy Habsburg hips. Lo and behold, Marie-Louise produced a baby boy (the King of Rome) in short order. Napoleon was ecstatic – he finally had an heir to carry on his newfound imperial dynasty. (Never mind that said dynasty collapsed a few years later and his "heir" lived and died in exile – the poor kid never got to rule a day – but hey, the best-laid plans of emperors and diapers often go awry.)

Sometimes the drama came not from lack of children, but *delays* in producing them. Take the case of Louis XVI of France and Marie Antoinette – a royal couple whose bedroom issues became the talk of every court in Europe. They married as awkward teenagers and, in an era when a royal marriage was expected to *ahem* bear fruit within a year or two, this pair kept everyone waiting seven long years before consummating the marriage and having a child. You can imagine the scandalized whispers in Versailles: "Are they doing it right? Is the King… um… capable? Is the Queen too frigid?" Pamphlets and gossips speculated wildly – was Louis XVI impotent or just clueless? (Modern historians suggest possibly a minor medical issue or simple youthful nerves.) Eventually, with some coaching from Marie Antoinette's brother (yes, her brother awkwardly gave Louis XVI bedroom advice), the couple sorted things out and had their first daughter, then a son. But that *seven-year itch* period put tremendous strain on them, with pressure from both their families. Marie Antoinette's mother (Empress Maria Theresa) wrote stern letters basically saying "Get on with it, daughter – produce an heir for France!" The whole ordeal shows how even natural procreation, usually a private matter, was a public mission for royals – complete with progress reports to meddling relatives and diplomats.

All this obsession with heirs turned what should be a joyous family milestone – the birth of a child – into a high-stakes drama. A royal delivery room was filled not just with midwives but with the weight of expectation. When a prince was born, church bells rang and nations rejoiced; if a princess arrived instead, there was often an audible collective sigh (and perhaps a tactful, "We'll get 'em next time" toast at court).

94

Queens were known to apologize for giving birth to daughters, as if they'd let down the team. Kings, for their part, would grumble and immediately start planning the next attempt, as if conception were a military campaign that had suffered a temporary setback. It's hard to overstate how absurd the pressure could become. In some realms, they even had *protocols* for witnessing royal births to ensure the baby was legit – imagine government ministers literally hovering at the door of the birthing chamber to verify the royal infant's gender and vitality, then sprinting off to announce it. Not exactly a warm, intimate family moment.

And if no heir came at all? Historically, that spelled disaster: rival factions might seize the chance to grab power, or foreign powers might interfere. The fear of a vacant throne was so serious that it led to wars, dissolutions of kingdoms, or new dynasties being imported. (Hello, Hanoverians in Britain – thanks to Queen Anne's lack of surviving heirs, Britain had to import a German prince as King George I in 1714, since literally *none* of Anne's 17 pregnancies yielded an heir who lived. The poor woman endured 18 child losses including infants and miscarriages, a personal tragedy and a dynastic crisis rolled into one.)

In short, the royal baby fever was no joke. It was a pressure cooker environment that strained marriages to the brink. Intimacy became a state duty, and each pregnancy was basically a roll of the dice with enormous political consequences. So, the next time you're at a family gathering and Aunt Mildred pesters you about when you'll have kids, be glad you're not a 16th-century queen – at least your nosy relatives can't spark a civil war if you don't produce a son by next summer. For these kings and queens, the cradle was truly the kingdom's fate, and that made the business of baby-making anything but fun or private. No wonder some of them lost their heads – some literally – over the stress of the heir apparent.

"An Heir and a Spare": Sibling Rivalry by Design

If you think *your* sibling rivalry is bad, wait until you hear about the royal "heir and spare" dynamic. In most royal families, one kid gets a crown and the others get a complex. The tradition for centuries has been to have at least two children – *"an heir and a spare"*, as the old saying goes – meaning if Child #1 (the heir) tragically kicks the bucket or proves incompetent, Child #2 can step up to bat. On paper, it's a sensible contingency plan. In practice, it's a recipe for epic sibling drama. Imagine growing up knowing your very existence is as a backup – you're literally the insurance policy for the throne. Some spares handled this with grace and found meaningful roles. But many a royal spare developed a knack for trouble: idle hands plus a royal allowance can lead to scandal, mischief, or even the occasional attempted coup at the dinner table (holidays at Windsor or Versailles sometimes made Thanksgiving with the in-laws look tame by comparison).

History is full of flamboyant *spares* who couldn't resist *testing* the heir. Often, the heir was the buttoned-up golden child raised to rule, while the spare had more freedom to rebel – and boy, did they use it. The result? Centuries of delicious gossip and periodic civil wars. Let's start with a dramatic example from antiquity: Cleopatra of Egypt and her sibling rivals. Royal sibling feuds don't get bloodier or more bizarre than the

Ptolemy family saga. Upon their father's death, Cleopatra and her brother Ptolemy XIII were supposed to rule Egypt jointly (and *eww*, as per custom, they were married to each other too). Spoiler: it didn't go well. By the time Cleopatra was in her early twenties, she and Ptolemy were literally at war – as in opposing armies battling for the crown. Their kid sister Arsinoe decided this looked like fun and declared herself queen as well, turning the feud into a three-way family throwdown. Cleopatra, being brilliant and ruthless, outmaneuvered her siblings by teaming up with Julius Caesar (with whom she famously also teamed up in... other ways). Caesar's military might helped Cleo defeat her brother; Ptolemy XIII ended up drowned in the Nile during the fighting, and Cleopatra regained the throne. Not done yet, she then had her pesky sister Arsinoe exiled and later assassinated on the steps of a temple – delivered courtesy of Cleopatra's next powerful Roman lover, Mark Antony. As one ancient chronicler noted, Cleopatra eventually "put to death all her kindred, till no one near her in blood remained alive". Now *that's* sibling rivalry taken to the extreme. The Ptolemy family basically wrote the book on how rival royal siblings could make *Game of Thrones* look like a kiddie pool. When your family reunions require armed guards and a poison-taster, you know there are issues.

Most royal sibling rivalries weren't *quite* as murdery as Cleopatra's, but they were plenty contentious. Brothers and sisters of monarchs throughout history have played an endless game of "Why not me?" Consider the English crown: King Henry VIII (yes, him again) was actually a second son – the spare for his elder brother Prince Arthur. Only Arthur's early death made Henry the heir, changing the course of

British history. But go back a generation: King Richard the Lionheart (Richard I) and his younger brother Prince John (of Robin Hood fame) had a classic heir-spare tension. While Richard was off crusading heroically, John was the restless spare back home, stirring trouble. John *allegedly* plotted against Richard, tried to seize power in his absence, and was generally the scheming little brother from central casting. Once Richard died, John did become king – proving that sometimes the spare does inherit the crown, especially if he's done a bit of nefarious scheming on the side. The two brothers' story gave England years of turmoil and also a legend of folklore (wicked Prince John vs. noble King Richard). Talk about sibling issues writ large.

Another dramatic case: When William the Conqueror died in 1087, he decided to play a twisted joke on his sons. Instead of giving everything to the eldest (Robert Curthose), he split the inheritance – William II (middle son) got England, Robert got Normandy. Cue *immediate fraternal warfare*. The brothers literally fought a war over who should rule what, each convinced he was the rightful top dog. Their disputes, which legend says once started with Robert rebelling after William the Conqueror *spilled a chamber pot* on him (accidentally or not, who knows), led to years of conflict. Eventually the youngest brother, Henry, also jumped into the fray, seized the English throne, and later defeated Robert to snatch Normandy as well. So in this case, Spare #2 (Henry) outmaneuvered Spare #1 (Robert) *and* the original heir William II died in a mysterious hunting accident (possibly "arranged" – things were suspiciously Game-of-Thronesy). The Norman dynasty basically turned into a sibling squabble that shaped English history. Imagine Thanksgiving dinner if those three had to share a turkey – the wishbone tug-of-war might have turned lethal.

The concept of having a *"spare"* was supposed to ensure stability, but ironically it often introduced *volatility*. A spare with ambition is a dangerous thing. Sometimes they would actively conspire to *replace* the heir or even the reigning monarch. In the Ottoman Empire, they didn't mess around with hopeful "spare" princes – they preemptively solved the problem in a rather gruesome way. Ottoman sultans historically practiced fratricide: upon ascending the throne, a new sultan would have his brothers (all of them) executed to prevent rival claims. It was an officially sanctioned practice – talk about cutthroat succession planning (literally). For instance, Sultan Mehmed III in 1595 invited his 19(!) brothers to a nice family gathering… and then had them strangled one by one with silk bowstrings. The youngest was only 11 years old. Yes, being a royal spare in Istanbul came with a shockingly short life expectancy. The logic was brutal: *no brother, no rival.* (Side benefit: no awkward birthday gifts to buy for 19 siblings.) Eventually, the Ottomans got squeamish and stopped the killings, opting to lock spares away in gilded cages (the *Kafes*) in the palace – luxurious house arrest for life, basically. Still, as far as sibling rivalry solutions go, that's… extreme. The very existence of such practices underscores how *dangerous* a rivalry between "the heir and the spare" could be in a monarchical system.

Even in places without sanctioned fratricide, the heir-spare dynamic caused plenty of family feuds. The British royal family offers some well-known modern examples. Queen Elizabeth II was the heir; her younger sister Princess Margaret grew up as the spare. While they loved each other, Margaret famously embraced a more rebellious, party-girl lifestyle that sometimes clashed with the Queen's dutiful image. Margaret once quipped, "Disobedience is my joy" – not exactly something Her Majesty could ever say. As the spare, Margaret didn't have a clear role and struggled to find purpose, leading to colorful episodes that fed the tabloids. Fast forward to the next generation: Prince Charles (heir) and Prince Andrew (spare until Charles had sons) also had vastly different reputations – Charles the serious workhorse, Andrew the playboy prince with a penchant for troublesome friendships (to put it mildly). And of course, in recent times we have the tale of Prince William and Prince Harry. William, as the heir to the current throne, shoulders the destiny of kingship; Harry, long branded the spare, spent years as the "fun" younger brother, known for cheeky antics and a rebellious streak. That dynamic eventually culminated in Harry spectacularly stepping away from royal duties altogether, moving across the ocean, and spilling the royal family tea in a memoir pointedly titled "Spare" (he *owned* the label). It doesn't involve battlefields or assassinations (thank goodness), but it shows the emotional toll of growing up second in line. Harry himself wrote that as the spare he felt like he was born just in case something happened to the heir – to provide "backup… or a spare part. Kidney, perhaps. Blood transfusion, speck of bone marrow…". When you're literally comparing yourself to an organ donor for your older brother, that's a royal complex if ever there was one!

Not all spare-heir relationships were antagonistic – some were marked by genuine affection and teamwork. There have been brothers who supported each other or sisters who were best friends. But the *potential* for rivalry was always there, baked into the hierarchy. Picture being the younger royal sibling watching your elder brother or sister groomed for greatness from day one – tutors, ceremonies, everyone bowing and scraping to the *future monarch* – while you get a polite pat on the head and maybe the governorship of a far-off island to keep you busy. It's bound to create some… tension. Often the spare had more leeway to be the wild child, which could either mean becoming a beloved, relatable figure – or a scandalous headache for the family. Some spares chose military careers to win glory since they couldn't have a throne (a lot of second sons became decorated generals or admirals). Others became known for *partying, gambling,* and extravagant spending – after all, they had a royal title without the crushing responsibility, a dangerous combination for the fiscally irresponsible. As one wit put it, when you're born second in line, you might spend a lifetime either searching for purpose… or plotting a palace coup over Thanksgiving dinner (metaphorically speaking).

Legendary instances of sibling strife abound: The Stanley brothers of the 15th century Wars of the Roses literally switched sides and betrayed each other during battle. The Stuart princes in 18th-century Britain, Charles Edward (Bonnie Prince Charlie) and Henry, quarreled over claims to the throne-in-exile. In Russia, Czar Peter the Great had to deal with his half-sister Sophia who acted as regent and didn't want to give up power – he eventually sent her to a convent after quashing her supporters. Even sisters got in on the act – Queen Mary I of England and her half-sister Elizabeth (later Elizabeth I) had a pretty toxic relationship for a while. Mary, a Catholic, at one point imprisoned the Protestant Elizabeth in the Tower of London on suspicions of intrigue. Elizabeth lived in constant fear for her life during Mary's reign. Not exactly the stuff of sisterly slumber parties. Only after Mary's death could Elizabeth breathe easy (and take the throne). So, even when they weren't directly fighting on a battlefield, heirs and spares could engage in psychological warfare and court intrigue that shaped nations.

The heir-spare setup was – and is – essentially *sibling rivalry by design*. By design, one sibling has clear priority, and the other has an ambiguous place. Sometimes that resulted in beautiful loyalty – the spare steadfastly supporting the heir (as the Queen Mother Elizabeth famously did for her brother-in-law King Edward VIII… until he abdicated and her husband became the unexpected heir, long story!). But just as often, it bred resentment or reckless behavior. As a result, royal parents historically were constantly playing referee (or jailer) between their kids. Medieval kings would dole out just enough land or titles to keep junior sons happy, but not enough to empower a rebellion – a delicate dance indeed. Queen mothers would implore their children to get along ("Please don't poison your brother at dinner, dear, that would upset Mama"). Despite such efforts, many royal family trees are littered with *feuding branches* and even a few severed limbs thanks to heir-vs-spare showdowns.

In the modern era, constitutional rules and media scrutiny have tamed the violent possibilities, but the emotional undercurrent is still there. The spare often struggles to define themselves outside their sibling's shadow. And the heir can feel burdened while watching the spare seemingly have more freedom. It's a dynamic as old as monarchy itself. So, the next time your sibling borrows your shirt without asking or slightly upstages you at a family event, be glad you're not royalty – at least they're not likely to march on your house with an army or conspire with foreign mercenaries to steal your inheritance. In the grand scheme of things, a little regular sibling bickering is *peanuts* compared to the palace intrigue of an heir and a spare at odds.

Regal Parenting (No Manual Provided)

Being a parent is hard enough, but raising a future monarch? That came with its own twisted rulebook – except nobody actually wrote the rulebook. Royal parenting for much of history was an odd mix of pampering luxury and emotional distance, with a healthy dose of protocol and a platoon of nannies. In effect, kings and queens outsourced 90% of the child-rearing to professionals, while they themselves performed parental duties about as often as they performed, say, *cooking dinner* (almost never). The result: some truly bizarre childhoods for princes and princesses, and plenty of heartache for royal moms and dads who were often more figureheads than nurturing caregivers to their kids.

In many royal households, the moment a princely baby exited the womb, the child was whisked away into the arms of waiting nurses, governesses, tutors – essentially a small army of employees tasked with turning that wriggling infant into a *proper monarch-in-training*. The queen or king might drop by for a photo op (or its historical equivalent, a quick dandling on the knee in front of courtiers), but the day-to-day *diaper duty* and lullabies? Not on the royal schedule. It was considered undignified for a reigning monarch or consort to be too hands-on with toddlers. After all, running a kingdom is a full-time job – who has time to change nappies when you're changing history? As a result, many royal children grew up seeing their parents in almost ceremonial contexts. One famous anecdote recounts how King George V (grandfather of Elizabeth II) once passed a nanny pushing a baby carriage in the palace and politely inquired, "Whose baby is that?" The nanny, one imagines with a stunned expression, replied: "It's yours, Sir." George V had failed to recognize his own infant son! That's how little interaction some kings had with their kids – literally not enough face time to know what they looked like in person.

Another oft-cited example of royal parenting chilliness is Queen Elizabeth II herself. When her young children (Prince Charles and Princess Anne) were small in the 1950s, Elizabeth – following tradition – left much of their daily care to nannies and governesses. She and Prince Philip would see the children for a short, scheduled meet-and-greet each day, almost like a very formal playdate. One staff member recalled that Her Majesty "would no more visit the nursery than fly – instead we took the children to see her each day" for a brief, poised encounter. And indeed, newsreels from that era show the little Prince Charles greeting his mother with a polite handshake after she returned from a long Commonwealth tour – the sort of frosty formality you'd expect between the Queen and a visiting dignitary, not mom and her 5-year-old. It wasn't that Elizabeth didn't *love* her kids – by all accounts she did, and later in life she reportedly regretted not being more present – but she had inherited a very stiff upper lip approach to parenting. Emotion was reined in; duty came first. Hugs were scarce. (Princess Diana, a generation later, would famously rebel against this style, hugging her boys publicly and insisting on being a hands-on mum – but that was a mini-revolution in royal behavior.)

Historically, such distance was the norm. Going back further, many royal mothers – especially queens consort – had no say in their children's upbringings once the babies were born. The children belonged to the *State* more than to their parents, in a sense. One extreme case was Empress Catherine the Great of Russia. When Catherine gave birth to her son, the future Tsar Paul I, she barely got to hold him before he was taken away. Her husband's aunt, Empress Elizabeth (then the reigning ruler), literally snatched the newborn prince and announced she would raise him herself, sidelining Catherine entirely. Catherine, exhausted from childbirth, watched in horror as her baby was carried off. She didn't see her son again for *weeks*, and thereafter only on rare scheduled visits – once a month, then once every few months. Empress Elizabeth's chilling message to Catherine was essentially: "Thank you for producing *Russia's child*. We'll take it from here." Catherine wrote of her heartbreak and anger – she had been reduced to a mere *broodmare*, her son reared by others and taught to view his mother with suspicion. The psychological toll on both mother and child was huge: Catherine and Paul's relationship was always strained (he grew up resenting her, and she, perhaps unconsciously, resented him being used as a political tool). It's a sad example of how royal protocol could override basic parental bonds.

A similar story unfolded in Britain a couple centuries earlier: Queen Anne of Denmark, wife of James I (VI of Scotland), had her first son, Henry, essentially confiscated by the state apparatus. James insisted the baby heir be given his own household at Stirling Castle to be raised by appointed lords, far from Mom. Anne was furious. She *begged* to be allowed more access to her son, but James and the Scottish council refused. Anne even threatened at one point "not to bear any more children" if she wasn't permitted to raise Prince Henry herself – basically a royal motherhood strike! (That's a pretty gutsy ultimatum to give a king: *Let me see my baby or no more heirs from me.*) In the end, a compromise was reached: Henry stayed in the aristocratic nursery, but Anne was allowed a bit more say for future kids. Still, she never got to be the kind of mother she wanted to be for Henry. This shows how even queens regnant or consort had to wrestle with court traditions that saw royal children as "property" of the realm, to be shaped by governors, tutors, and councils rather than by Mommy and Daddy.

For those royal children "lucky" enough to live with their parents in the same palace, things could still be oddly distant. Often the nursery or children's wing was physically far from the state rooms – sometimes at the opposite end of a vast palace. This meant that in times of crisis, kids could literally be forgotten. There's a darkly comic anecdote from 1620 about King Frederick V of Bohemia and Queen Elizabeth (Stuart): when their palace in Prague was under attack and they had to flee, they managed to evacuate with their many children – or so they thought. Only after they'd nearly left did a courtier doing a last sweep of the rooms hear a baby's cries. He discovered the royals had accidentally left behind their

11-month-old son, Prince Rupert, who had been forgotten by a panicked nurse! Imagine the parenting guilt on that carriage ride ("Honey, do we have all the kids? ... Wait, where's the baby?! TURN AROUND!"). Little Prince Rupert was rescued at the last minute, thankfully. But such an incident underscores that royal kids were often out of sight, out of mind, tucked away in remote nurseries with servants.

Speaking of servants, the royal nanny was one of the most powerful people in the palace, at least from the child's perspective. These nannies and governesses could practically *supplant* the parents in affection and influence. Many a royal mother felt jealous of how attached her children became to a beloved nanny. And some royal fathers and mothers were frankly content with that arrangement – it spared them the work. Day-to-day child-rearing was seen as *messy business* best left to underlings. Wet nurses breastfed the infants (it was considered unbecoming for a queen to nurse her own child). Then stern governesses took over, enforcing etiquette and discipline. The goal was to produce miniature adults – impeccably behaved young princes and princesses who could curtsey, converse in three languages, and sit through long ceremonies without picking their noses. Childhood play and coddling were often in short supply. One historian noted that royal parents were obsessed with making their kids grow up as soon as possible, sometimes forcing an unnatural maturity that backfired later. (The quote was that this method "came at a cost" – indeed, some royal offspring who never got to be *kids* ended up with stunted emotional development. Ironically, princes kept from playing "pretend" as toddlers sometimes grew up to make terrible, immature decisions as adults – who'd have guessed?)

Discipline could be harsh as well. Take King George II of Britain – he as a child was reportedly *caned* by his governess and grew up fearing his father. In fact, there's a famous line: *"My father was frightened of his father, I was frightened of my father, and I am damned well going to see to it that my children are frightened of me"*, said by George V describing the cycle of royal parenting. Yikes. The House of Hanover (18th-19th century British royals) had a reputation for terrible parent-child relationships – one courtier quipped that the Hanoverian kings "like ducks, produce bad parents... They trample on their young." It was not far off. King George III famously had awful rows with his eldest son (the future George IV), essentially hating each other. George III's father, Frederick, had been estranged from *his* father, George II. It was almost a family tradition: each generation of Hanoverian dads and sons loathed each other with a passion. Distance and formality certainly didn't help those relationships. When your dad is more of a stern monarch than a loving papa, teenage rebellion is bound to be extreme (and in the case of the Georges, it involved parliamentary factions and press smear campaigns – the teen angst of a prince can rock an entire nation).

Royal mothers could likewise be distant or tightly constrained by protocol. One poignant example: Queen Isabella of Castile dearly loved her daughter Catherine of Aragon (the same Catherine who later had the misfortune of being Henry VIII's first wife). When Catherine was stranded in England as a young widow, effectively held against her will, Isabella wrote heartbroken letters saying "we cannot endure that a daughter whom we love should be so far from us when she is in affliction". But due to politics, Isabella couldn't simply fetch her daughter home. Royal children, even once grown, were pieces on the political chessboard – marriage alliances and diplomacy often meant parents and children spent years apart, missing each other terribly while maintaining stoic appearances.

The blend of pampering and neglect in royal childhoods was truly bizarre. On one hand, young princes and princesses lived in luxury that other children could only dream of: jeweled rattles, gilded cribs, ponies as playthings, tutors teaching them fine arts and fencing. They were literally *waited on hand and foot*. If a royal kid sneezed, ten people might leap to attention with handkerchiefs. But on the other hand, these same royal kids might rarely get a simple hug from Mum or a game of catch with Dad. They were often lonely, emotionally starved in the middle of a court teeming with people. The Queen of Bohemia's daughter, Princess Sophia, once bitterly noted that her mother "preferred the sight of her monkeys and dogs to that of her children." Ouch. (Queen Elizabeth of Bohemia *did* have a beloved menagerie of pets she doted on. Imagine being a kid peeking around the door hoping for a cuddle, only to see Mom cooing over a lapdog instead. A royal palace, yet no warmth for the actual offspring – no wonder Sophia grew up to write that burn.)

Sometimes, royal parents *did* feel genuine anguish about this setup but felt unable to change it. They were trapped in tradition. For instance, Queen Marie Antoinette of France, in the late 18th century, *bucked* the trend by insisting on spending time with her children and allowing them a more normal childhood. She even let them play and didn't constantly remind them of their status. "Our children learn soon enough what they are," she said, determined to let them be kids for a while. This was considered radical at the time – some courtiers were shocked that she would, say, sit on the floor playing with her children or dress them in simpler clothes rather than mini-royal regalia. Marie Antoinette's approach was an Enlightenment-influenced one, treating her kids with affection and informality (she called them "friends"). Unfortunately, her enemies spun this as her being a frivolous, neglectful queen (one pamphlet even depicted her as ignoring state affairs to play with her children – imagine that, a mother spending time with her kids, how scandalous!). She was ahead of her time, but her efforts show that even in the most formal courts, parental love could surface and push against the boundaries of protocol.

In other cases, royals learned the hard way that delegating all parenting wasn't great. Queen Victoria adored her nine children but wasn't the most cuddly of moms – she found babies "rather disgusting" and left their upbringing mostly to governesses. However, she projected an image of a happy domestic queen to set a moral example (the whole "mother of Europe" image, with portraits of her with a brood of kids on her lap – carefully staged, of course). Her children later had mixed feelings about their childhood, and Victoria herself confessed she wasn't a fan of being pregnant or dealing with toddlers. She once warned her own daughter about being *too* attentive a mother, oddly believing that overly watching the children could spoil them or create problems later. This might explain why some of Victoria's children, like Edward VII, grew up as playboys once free of the nursery – maybe a little more "watching" might have helped!

There were also instances where royal parents were surprisingly close and affectionate, though these tend to be the exceptions and often tragically ended. The last Russian Tsar, Nicholas II, and his wife Alexandra, doted on their five children and kept them very close – a stark contrast to their predecessors. Alexandra wrote, "The greatest treasure that parents can leave their children is a happy childhood," and she meant it. She and Nicholas spent as much time as possible with their four grand duchess daughters and young son Alexei. They played, read bedtime stories, even allowed the kids to sleep in their room when they were scared. They were so *hands-on* that one of their nannies complained the Empress popped into the nursery *too often* – she was fired for grumbling about the parents wanting to see their own kids!. Now *that's* an upside-down scenario for royals. The Romanov children by all accounts adored their Papa and Mama. But the flip side: the kids were *overprotected* and isolated from the world, which didn't help them understand the changing times – and it certainly didn't save them from the grim fate of the Russian Revolution. Nonetheless, it's poignant to see that even in that ill-fated family, the instinct to give their children a warm upbringing broke through the stiff court norms.

By the 20th century, royal parenting began catching up (ever so slowly) with common-sense human parenting. The current British royals, for example, have largely done away with the "seen and not heard" philosophy for kids. Prince William and Princess Kate kneel down to talk to their children eye-to-eye at public events (cue gasps from old-timers). They've been seen hugging and laughing with their kids in ways that would make Queen Mary roll in her grave. They are still constrained in some ways (certain traditions and boarding school at 8 years old remain, for better or worse), but they consciously try to be more present and emotionally available. This shift largely began with Princess Diana, who insisted on taking her boys William and Harry to McDonald's and amusement parks, and hugging them whenever she pleased – a stark change from the formality of previous generations. Diana famously said she wanted her sons to have a normal life and not grow up emotionally stunted by palace protocols, as many before them had.

In summary, regal parenting through history often followed the mantra: *delegate everything.* Royal couples had to navigate or negotiate how their children would be raised amid stiff court customs. Many just went along with tradition, resulting in kids who called their nanny "Mama" and had to schedule appointments to see their actual parents. Some royal mothers (like Catherine the Great, Queen Anne of Denmark, etc.) fought back against these customs to little avail, suffering personal sorrow as a result. The combination of lavish care (education, comfort) and emotional neglect was a hallmark of palace childhoods. It created heirs who were sometimes worryingly detached or rebellious, and spares who were adrift (or too *adrift* in mischief). Perhaps the strangest thing is that for all the privilege, many a royal child would likely have traded their gilded rocking horse for a few more bedtime stories read by Mom or Dad.

Royal couples had to put on a united front in public as majestic parents, while privately they might disagree fiercely about child-rearing or feel hurt at being kept at arm's length from their own kids. Few things create more domestic tension than parenting differences – now imagine those differences playing out in a *castle* with a bureaucracy involved! Some kings blamed their queens for how the kids turned out; some queens blamed the system that wouldn't let them mother properly. It was, truly, a no-manual, no-win situation at times. And as we'll see next, the stresses of succession and parenting combined could amplify marital strife in tragic ways.

Succession Stress and Domestic Mess

If you thought the story ends once the royal bundle of joy is born, think again. In many ways, that's when the real domestic mess began. The business of producing and educating heirs tended to pour gasoline on any flickers of marital tension that already existed – and light a match for good measure. Royal couples under succession pressure often found their personal relationships strained to the breaking point by issues like the baby's gender, health, and personality, or by the sheer trauma of multiple pregnancies and losses. In the palace nursery, hope and fear lived side by side, and occasionally farce made an appearance too. It was a crucible where the royal couple's anxieties, expectations, and egos all got projected onto a drooling toddler in a tiny crown.

First off, let's talk gender drama. We've already seen how not having a male heir was the bane of many a queen's existence. When a baby arrived and – *oh no* – it was a girl instead of the long-awaited boy, the blame games commenced. Kings, courtiers, even the common folk might subtly (or not so subtly) cast aspersions on the queen: "She failed to bear a son." The irony that it was actually the father's chromosomes deciding that outcome was lost on them. Instead, wives felt immense guilt and husbands often felt, frankly, cheated. This led to some very frosty royal bedrooms. Marital intimacy became less about love and more a grim duty to try again for *the right result*. For example, Henry VIII (yes, him one last time) notoriously reacted to each daughter born as if it were a personal insult. After Princess Mary was born and no sons followed, Henry grew distant from Catherine of Aragon and eventually decided to replace her. When Anne Boleyn gave birth to Princess Elizabeth, Henry reportedly told someone that if it was a girl this time, surely boys would follow – trying to keep optimistic – but privately he was stewing. (Anne's subsequent miscarriages of male fetuses absolutely sealed her doom; Henry's disappointment curdled into accusations of witchcraft and adultery, as if to rationalize why she hadn't given him a boy.) These gender expectations turned what should be a loving environment for a newborn into a source of *palpable stress*. Imagine being a queen recovering from childbirth and knowing your spouse is sulking because the baby's the "wrong" sex – it's heartbreaking and infuriating. Some queens like Catherine of Aragon even said as much; Catherine after one stillbirth apologized in a letter for "displeasing" Henry by not providing a living son – a tragic reflection of how she internalized the blame.

Even once an heir (male) was secured, the pressure didn't let up. In fact, it simply shifted to ensuring that heir survived and was suitably prepared. Infant mortality was high in earlier eras, and royal infants were not exempt. The death of a royal child could be devastating personally and destabilizing politically. Couples that suffered the loss of children often either grew closer in grief or, just as often, saw their marriage crack under the sorrow and *implicit blame*. Queen Anne and her husband Prince George endured 18 child losses (miscarriages, stillbirths, babies and young children). It bound them in shared tragedy – they were reportedly devoted to each other through it all, leaning on each other for comfort – but it left Anne depressed and the Stuart dynasty without an heir, causing a succession crisis. By contrast, some royal husbands grew bitter at their wives if children kept dying, as though it were the mother's failure. One French king, Louis XII, after losing an infant, cruelly joked that maybe God didn't want his queen to have a son. Not exactly supportive grief counseling from that husband. The emotional fallout of repeated miscarriages could be severe. Queens felt pressure to try again and again, turning them into perpetual expectant mothers or mourners (or both). King Philip II of Spain, for instance, cycled through four wives in part because of infant losses – each time a wife died or failed to produce surviving sons, he'd marry another princess. It's as if the wives were deemed interchangeable incubators in the quest for an heir – a grim reality that certainly didn't lend itself to marital bliss.

Then there's the issue of the heir's upbringing and personality, which could become a battlefield for the parents. If the heir was sickly or disabled, parents might secretly panic or blame each other for "bad blood." A classic example: Tsar Alexei, the only son of Nicholas II and Alexandra of Russia, was born with hemophilia (a blood disorder). The parents were devastated and terrified of losing him (hemophilia was often fatal in that era). Alexandra, desperate to keep Alexei alive, turned to the faith-healer Rasputin – whose influence in court affairs caused enormous friction and scandal. Nicholas and Alexandra's once loving marriage also endured strain as they isolated themselves to care for Alexei. They hid his illness, fretted constantly, and in doing so made decisions that ultimately contributed to public distrust. All of that from the simple fact of having a sickly heir. In earlier times, a physically weak heir was a huge liability – it could invite challengers and erode confidence in the dynasty. So parents sometimes went overboard trying to "toughen up" a delicate child, or conversely coddled them excessively. Neither approach was great for the marriage if the king and queen disagreed on it. One might say "Let him rest, he's unwell," the other "No, he must train harder to be strong!" – cue marital arguments in the royal bedchamber.

If the heir or spare had a rebellious or difficult personality, that too was a source of woe. King Henry II of England had a truly rotten time with his sons. Despite giving them lands and titles, *three out of four* of Henry's surviving sons ended up rebelling against him in one form or another. Talk about ungrateful kids – they literally waged war on Dad! This caused enormous marital strife between Henry II and his queen, Eleanor of Aquitaine, who at one point sided with her sons against her husband. Henry, furious, imprisoned Eleanor for years. The family was a powder keg of clashing egos. One can only imagine the dinner conversation at Henry II's court: "Pass the salt... and by the way, Father, I'm in open revolt against you. Please don't ask Mother what she's plotting." In a more domestic sense, whenever a royal child misbehaved or went off the rails, the parents might blame each other: "He's wild because you spoiled him!" "No, he's angry because you ignore him!" – the same arguments regular parents have, but with higher stakes. In the Hanoverian era, King George II and his wife Caroline had very differing views on their eldest son Frederick. They ended up despising him, and he them – a poisonous triangle. Caroline once said she hoped she'd outlive Frederick because "he'd ruin everything." George II outright celebrated when Frederick died before inheriting the throne (not a shining moment of fatherhood). Such was the breakdown that it clearly put strain on George and Caroline's partnership, having a son they both disliked so much.

Sometimes the spare caused domestic strife by being troublesome. A "problem child" who wasn't the heir could still embarrass the family. For instance, George V and Queen Mary had an heir (Edward VIII) and a spare (George VI). The heir turned out to be the rebellious one – Edward VIII later abdicated for Wallis Simpson – but earlier on, another spare of that generation, Prince George (the King's younger son), was a playboy and had *scandals* (drugs, affairs) that worried his parents. King George V reportedly lamented that his children were "all failures except maybe Bertie" (the future George VI). So even if the crown is secure, a wayward spare can cause husband and wife to fret and feud over how to handle it. Do we cover it up? Punish them? Marry them off quickly to settle them down? These debates could get heated.

One almost farcical dimension in royal nurseries was the tendency of kings and queens to project all their anxieties and hopes onto a tiny child. If you think modern helicopter parents are intense, picture a king determined that his toddler son carry the weight of national destiny on his chubby shoulders. Some royal couples would obsess over every sign – "The prince sneezed! Is he getting sick? Fetch the physician – oh no, what if he's weak?!" or "The little princess frowned at the portrait of our ancestor – does she lack proper respect? Are we raising a rebel?" It sounds absurd, but these people lived under constant pressure to mold the perfect future monarch. They sometimes robbed their kids of normal childhood in the process, turning the nursery into a miniature court. Toddlers were dressed in elaborate finery and expected to sit through ceremonies without crying. (Good luck with that – there are accounts of young heirs throwing royal tantrums during long coronation church services, leading to much parental mortification and undoubtedly some blaming behind closed doors.)

A great comedic image is the royal parents fussing while a toddler prince runs around with a toy sceptre, bonking courtiers on the knee. The king might laugh nervously – "Oh look, he's practicing ruling!" – while the queen is horrified – "Don't encourage him, he just whacked the Lord Chamberlain's gouty foot!" Deep down, they worry: Will he grow up to be a tyrant? Too soft? Too rash? They see portents in every nursery game. And because the stakes are high (this little kid will one day rule us all), everyone from the governess to the prime minister also has an opinion on the child's upbringing. The pressure on the royal couple to "get it right" with raising the heir could drive them up the wall. Disagreements on education were common. One parent might favor a strict military tutor, the other a humanist scholarly tutor. One might want the child to bond with common children for empathy; the other recoils at the idea of the heir playing with commoners' kids. These arguments were not just theoretical – they determined the character of the next monarch, so factions at court would even side with one parent or the other's philosophy. King James II and his first wife quarreled over how Catholic vs. Protestant to raise their daughters – which had huge political implications and also no doubt caused personal friction.

And what if the heir turned out to have *ideas of their own* that the parents didn't like? That could really amp up tensions. Imagine being a king and your heir says, "Dad, when I'm king I'm going to undo that policy you care about." Awkward! This happened: Emperor Peter the Great of Russia had a son, Alexei, who disliked Peter's westernizing reforms and basically wanted to rollback everything his father did. Peter, a rather unforgiving fellow, ultimately suspected his son of treason – and had Alexei imprisoned and tortured to death in 1718. Yes, he *killed his own adult son*. One can scarcely call that a "parenting disagreement" – that's outright elimination. But it stemmed from a fundamental rift in values between father and heir. On a less fatal level, even enlightened monarchs like Emperor Franz Joseph of Austria had trouble with their heirs – his son Rudolf clashed with him on politics and ended up tragically in a murder-suicide pact (Mayerling incident), devastating the family. In England, George III's American policies were hated by his heir George IV, who privately sympathized with the Americans – leading to massive rows in palace halls. The stress of knowing your own child opposes you can put a royal marriage under strain too, as each parent may take sides or handle it differently (one might coddle the child, the other crack down).

Amid all this serious stuff, there were moments of unintentional comedy. Court diaries tell of young princes escaping their tutors and sliding down palace banisters while frantic attendants gave chase – with the king and queen perhaps secretly amused but officially disapproving. One French Dauphin in the 1600s loved to sneak into the kitchens to eat pastries, infuriating his strict dietician and causing his parents to fret he'd get chubby (oh the scandal of a plump heir!). In one case, a royal child was seen riding a pet donkey through the formal gardens during an important diplomatic visit – the king had to stifle a laugh and later scold the child while the queen face-palmed. These incidents, while minor, could actually spark arguments: "You indulge him too much!" "Oh, let him be a boy!" – that eternal parental divide between discipline and letting kids be kids, played out on a grand stage.

In the end, the palace nursery was indeed a crucible of high hopes and deep fears for royal couples. It magnified their unity or exposed their rifts. A successful production of a healthy heir could cement a marriage (at least for a time) – *we did it!* – while repeated failures or troubles could drive a wedge the size of a coronation throne between husband and wife. Some royal marriages survived these pressures intact, even strengthened (shared purpose and all). Others cracked under the combined weight of public expectation and private heartbreak. We've seen queens discarded for not meeting heir quotas, kings humiliated by rebellious offspring, and royal parents who barely got to know their own kids. Perhaps the biggest lesson from all these heirs, spares, and parenting nightmares is a human one: at the end of the day, kings and queens were parents too – flawed, hopeful, anxious, sometimes loving, sometimes disastrously clumsy. They had to learn (or sometimes failed to learn) that children aren't just mini-monarchs to be crafted like state projects; they're individuals who need love, guidance, and yes, the freedom to be kids. And when parents – royal or not – lose sight of that, it's a recipe for family drama.

So as our regal couples closed the nursery doors each night, perhaps they breathed a sigh of relief and a prayer: *Please let our heir be healthy and our spare be loyal; let us have the wisdom not to mess them up too badly.* And maybe a nanny or two muttered under her breath: *Let the sovereigns remember, at least for a few minutes, that they're also mom and dad.* In the grand theater of monarchy, the curtains would fall on the day's intrigues – and in the nursery, a toddler would chew on a toy sceptre, blissfully unaware of the kingdom of expectations resting upon those tiny shoulders.

Chapter 7

The Spotlight and the Shadows – Media, Myths, and Privacy

Royal life has always been a grand performance on the world stage – complete with dazzling spotlights and plenty of shadows lurking just offstage. When the cameras roll, kings and queens wave serenely from balconies, projecting fairy-tale perfection. But once the curtains fall, they're as human as the rest of us – bickering over breakfast, tripping over the corgi, maybe even squabbling about whose turn it is to change the royal baby's diaper. In this chapter, we take a witty, no-holds-barred tour through how monarchs have juggled their public image and private realities. From centuries-old court gossips whispering in gilded halls to Twitter-era tabloid scandals, we'll see that the royal *"happily ever after"* is often as carefully edited as a Hollywood rom-com. It's a tale of two worlds: the spotlight that demands an impeccable myth, and the shadows where the truth – messy, ridiculous, and utterly human – resides. So grab your popcorn (or your tea and crumpets), and let's peek behind the palace curtains.

Court Gossip to Tabloid Fodder

Long before Netflix binges and 24/7 news feeds, royal couples were the *original* public entertainment. Think of pre-modern court gossip as a sort of medieval TMZ (minus the paparazzi vans). In the grand palaces of yore, court insiders would trade scandalous whispers about the king's quarrels with the queen over, say, her *extravagant* new wig or his wandering eye. These hushed rumors would waft through Versailles or Buckingham like the scent of over-perfumed courtiers. In 18th-century France, for example, pamphleteers known as *libellistes* cranked out illicit leaflets spilling the *royal tea* across Europe. They gleefully exaggerated – or outright fabricated – tales of marital discord and naughty bedroom antics among the Bourbon royals. Poor Marie Antoinette, in particular, was a frequent target. Slanderous pamphlets painted her as a scandalous flirt and worse; the number of pornographic libelles about her *proliferated* as the revolution neared. One can imagine peasants gobbling up these salacious stories by candlelight, *gasping* at every invented detail of the Queen's alleged affairs. In short, before the internet existed, fake news about queens doing shocking things was already going viral (via horse-and-carriage distribution).

In 1820, a satirical cartoon mocked a royal marriage on the rocks: "from two huge green bags, pear-shaped and broad-based, emerge the heads of the King and Queen," lampooning the estranged George IV and Queen Caroline. Even back then, royal domestic drama was front-page (or rather, pamphlet-page) fodder.

Fast forward to today, and the royal rumor mill is *alive and kicking* – only now it's supercharged by tabloids, Twitter, and clickbait headlines with all-caps and exclamation marks. Modern media eagerly scrutinize every micro-gesture of a royal couple for signs of trouble. Did a queen consort shoot her king a subtle side-eye at the state dinner? Cue the screaming front-page scandal! (Heaven forbid Her Majesty scowls at an undercooked dessert – tomorrow's headline might read: "ROYAL SPAT AT BANQUET: Queen's Icy Glare Sends King to Doghouse!") In fact, even a fleeting exchange can set off frenzy. When Kate Middleton and Queen Camilla exchanged a brief *"can you believe this?"* glance during a long sermon at Prince Harry's wedding, the internet went wild dissecting the "side-eye" seen 'round the world. One fan tweeted, *"That Kate Middleton side-eye!"*, as if decoding secret Morse code of marital discord. It's a reminder that public fascination with royal drama is nothing new – the medium has evolved from whispered rumors in drawing rooms to viral GIFs on social media, but the *audience appetite* remains the same. We, the public, simply cannot resist peeking at the gilded soap opera of kings and queens, be it through a 1700s pamphlet or a 2020s Instagram feed.

And let's be honest, royal couples have always given us *plenty* to gossip about. From Henry VIII's six wives (the Tudor version of a juicy reality show – "The Real Housewives of Tudor England," anyone?) to the flashy squabbles of modern Windsor dynasties, there has always been an eager market for tales of *palace intrigues*. The key difference now is speed and scale: what once took months to gossip across a kingdom now goes global in seconds. Yet as we'll see, no matter the century, the *plotlines* stay familiar – love, power, jealousy, and occasionally a well-aimed goblet of wine hurled in frustration (purely speculative…but one imagines it's happened). Royal couples, it turns out, have been living in a fishbowl for ages. The walls of that fishbowl may be made of stained glass and surrounded by guards, but everyone's still peering in, waiting for the next scandalous splash.

Image Crafting 101

Given that perpetual public gaze, it's no wonder modern monarchies have turned **image-crafting** into an art form (and a full-time job). Today's royal households boast entire communications teams whose sole mission is to present the royals as the happiest, most wholesome family in the realm – even if reality is…well, a tad less rosy. Welcome to *Image Crafting 101*, where every holiday portrait has perfect lighting and zero tantrums, every public outing is choreographed like a Broadway show, and every smile is calibrated to convey maximum marital bliss.

Take Britain's House of Windsor, masters of the "ideal family" brand. They release glossy Christmas card photos each year featuring coordinated outfits, adorable children, and typically at least one dog to up the cuteness factor. The unspoken message: *"See? We royals are just a normal, ridiculously photogenic family!"* At charity events, you'll spot united fronts – kings and queens holding hands, patting each other's back supportively, maybe even exchanging an inside joke for the cameras. (Never mind if they had a screaming match in the car beforehand about who left the palace without their reading glasses.) Public displays of affection are carefully metered: a gentle arm around the waist here, a loving gaze there. It's all part of cultivating that storybook image of a fairytale marriage. In fact, royal approval ratings often hinge on maintaining this picture-perfect facade. After all, many citizens may never meet their monarchs in person – their impression comes from those smiling balcony waves and happy family scenes on TV.

But pulling off a perpetual fairytale is a high-wire act worthy of the Cirque du Soleil. One wobble, one slip, and the illusion can come crashing down. The British royals famously abide by the mantra "never complain, never explain," which essentially means *"keep calm and carry on – with a smile."* So even if a king is furious at a tabloid lie or a princess is hurt by a public snub, they will usually endure it silently, lips sealed in that trademark polite grin. Complaining publicly or (gasp) explaining oneself would break the mystique. Instead, the royal strategy is to out-smile the scandal – pretend it doesn't bother them, and hope the public plays along. This works…until it doesn't. There's a constant tension between authenticity and appearance. Royals are expected to be *genuine* and relatable, yet also flawless. They must appear warm and "just like us," but also uphold an almost superhuman decorum. No pressure, Your Majesties!

Of course, even palace PR wizards sometimes stumble. For every image-control triumph – say, the late Queen Elizabeth II charming millions with a surprise comedy skit taking tea with Paddington Bear (a PR masterstroke that showcased her humor) – there's a PR disaster that reminds us the "perfect" image is, in fact, a mirage. Consider the case of Catherine, Princess of Wales (Kate Middleton), in 2024. As rumors swirled about her prolonged absence from the public eye due to a health issue, the palace released a seemingly sweet Mother's Day photo of Kate with her children. Problem: the image was so obviously Photoshopped that internet sleuths noticed wonky details (like a mysteriously blurry hand and oddly patterned hair) within minutes. Busted! Kate even issued a personal apology for the doctored pic, admitting she "got carried away" editing it – a rare royal mea culpa. The whole episode backfired spectacularly, fueling *more* speculation that the palace was covering something up. Media outlets declared it a "Streisand effect" fiasco, where trying to suppress gossip only amplified it. As one analyst noted, posting an egregiously edited "happy family" photo drew *more* attention and ridicule than if they had said nothing at all. Image crafting, meet reality.

Then there are the *staged photo-ops* that seemed like a good idea at the time...until they weren't. Royals have tried everything to burnish the family brand – sometimes to absurd effect. We've seen princes awkwardly grilling burgers at public barbecues to seem like down-to-earth dads, or queens donning casual jeans for "relatable" photos (cue tabloids cooing, "They're just like us!"). But if the choreography is too obvious, the public eye-roll is swift. One can't forget the utterly *cringe* moment when a palace press team set up a "spontaneous" family video of a royal couple cheerfully chatting with their kids – only for a behind-the-scenes outtake to leak, revealing a frustrated stage mom princess snapping *"We'll do it live!"* at a hapless assistant. So much for a candid home scene! The internet had a field day with that one, complete with memes of the royals as reality TV stars. The lesson? In the social media era, even a tightly controlled photo-op can explode in your face if any part of the mask slips. Royals must walk a fine line: be *charming* but not cheesy, *polished* but not plastic. It's a bit like watching someone juggle fine china – impressive, but you're half waiting for a plate to drop.

And yet, for all the choreographed perfection, we occasionally get a peek at the real personalities shining through – sometimes intentionally.

Queen Elizabeth's Paddington Bear skit we mentioned earlier was a huge hit precisely because it felt authentic and funny, showing a granny-with-a-marmalade-sandwich side of Her Majesty that endeared her to millions. Likewise, when a photo of King Felipe of Spain playfully piggybacking one of his giggling daughters made the rounds, people loved seeing the normally stoic monarch as a goofy dad for once. These *unscripted* (or seemingly unscripted) moments can humanize royals and actually boost their image. The paradox of image crafting is that sometimes the best PR is to let the mask drop *just a little*, intentionally, on your own terms – show the world a flash of genuine emotion or imperfection. Of course, as we'll see next, when the mask drops *unintentionally*, that's when the real fun – and fiasco – begins.

When the Mask Slips

No matter how expertly the royal PR machine operates, reality has a pesky way of intruding. The palace can script every public appearance down to the last curtsy, but they can't script *life*. Inevitably, there come those delicious (for us) moments when the regal mask slips – and suddenly the world sees the unscripted human behind it. For royal watchers, these moments are like Christmas and a soap opera finale rolled into one. For the royals' press secretaries, they're minor heart attacks. Let's explore a few classic instances when the carefully crafted image cracked, to satirical and sometimes serious effect.

Sometimes the slip is audible – a private remark caught on a hot mic that the royals never meant the public to hear. Exhibit A: then-Prince Charles, on a ski trip photo op in 2005, thought he was muttering under his breath about an annoying BBC reporter. The microphones, however, picked up every word. The future king sniped, *"Bloody people. I can't bear that man. He's so awful, he really is."* Oops! This unvarnished grumpiness – aimed at a journalist who had dared ask a question about Charles's upcoming wedding – was *not* part of the palace media plan. Here was the normally poised Prince of Wales sounding less like a fairy-tale prince and more like a cranky dad stuck in traffic. The headlines practically wrote themselves ("Churlish Charles!"), and palace spin doctors scrambled into damage control. Ironically, many Brits found the episode darkly funny and even a bit refreshing: *finally*, a genuine emotion! Still, you can bet every royal from London to Tokyo got a reminder memo after that: *"Assume every microphone is live, always."*

Then we have the bombshell tell-all interviews – the nuclear option for a disenchanted royal spouse who's done pretending everything is fine. Perhaps the most famous is Princess Diana's 1995 Panorama interview, where she calmly blew the lid off her failing marriage to Prince Charles. With a demure smile, Diana dropped a quotable grenade about Charles's longtime affair with Camilla: *"Well, there were three of us in this marriage, so it was a bit crowded."* Cue the collective gasp heard around the globe. In one sentence, the demure Princess of Wales confirmed the worst-kept secret in Britain and shattered the myth of the perfect prince and princess. She also spoke candidly about her misery behind palace doors – her postnatal depression, her bulimia, her feelings of isolation – all the struggles the royal PR machine had worked hard to hide. The impact was explosive: Diana's openness permanently changed how the public viewed the royal family, and it deeply rattled the "never complain" ethos at the palace.

Fast-forward a few decades, and we saw a redux of the royal tell-all with Meghan, Duchess of Sussex, giving her own candid interview in 2021. Meghan's revelations of feeling silenced and even suicidal within the royal fold (plus allegations of a racist comment by an unnamed family member) had Buckingham Palace in full-blown crisis mode, scrambling to respond without violating their beloved "no explanation" rule. These interviews are high-drama reminders that when a royal spouse decides to air the dirty linens, no amount of palace spin can contain the fallout. It's the ultimate mask drop – live on prime-time TV, with popcorn sold separately.

Leaked letters and illicit recordings have also fed the royal scandal mill, bridging the gap between *private* and *public* in the most cringe-worthy way. Imagine the palace aides' horror when intimate phone call transcripts between Prince Charles and Camilla (back in the 1980s, when both were married to other people) leaked to the press. The world suddenly learned far more than it ever wanted to about Charles's…ahem…personal fantasies (the infamous "tampon" comment still wins the TMI award of the century). That scandal, dubbed "Camillagate," was both mortifying and bizarrely comical – proof that even future monarchs shouldn't assume *any* conversation is secure. But such *whoopsies* aren't a strictly modern phenomenon. In the 18th century, love letters and secret correspondence sometimes found their way into the public domain to embarrass the crown. For instance, when King George IV tried to divorce his wildly popular wife, Queen Caroline, in 1820, *evidence* of her alleged infidelities (from spies and informants) was gathered in literal green bags. The public was so enthralled by the dirty laundry of that royal marriage that satirists seized the moment. A cartoon from that time shows the King and Queen as two oversized green bags (yes, bags with heads poking out) facing off – a visual representation that their baggage had become everyone's business. It's both savage and hilarious: the monarch of the world's mightiest empire reduced to a cartoon "old bag" for squabbling with his estranged wife. When the mask slips, the mighty truly can become the mocked.

And oh, the social media gaffes – a relatively new genre of royal slip-up, but one that's growing by the year. Royals are cautiously wading into platforms like Twitter and Instagram to connect with younger audiences. But the internet is a minefield. Case in point: a certain duchess (we won't name names, but her initials are M.M.) recently returned to Instagram and posted what looked like a breezy, off-the-cuff video. Except eagle-eyed fans noticed the reflections and background details suggested it took multiple tries to film that "casual" clip. Relatable? Sure – who among us *hasn't* reshot a selfie video 20 times? – but also a bit embarrassing for someone trying to appear effortlessly authentic. Then there was the time an official royal Twitter account accidentally tweeted a weird string of characters – as if a corgi walked over the keyboard – prompting a day of jokes about the Queen secretly sending coded messages on Twitter. (The palace dryly deleted the tweet and blamed a "technical error," but we prefer to imagine Her Majesty chuckling, "No, Philip, that's not how you do a hashtag.") Whether it's an accidental like on a controversial post, a photo posted with an unfiltered look at the palace interior (revealing, say, *way* too many wine bottles on the counter), or a royal staffer's Reddit AMA gone wrong, social media offers endless opportunities for the royal facade to spring a leak. The public eats it up, of course – every deleted tweet or awkward Instagram apology is another reminder that behind the titles and tiaras, these folks are fumbling through the digital age like the rest of us.

Each of these incidents – the hot mic grumble, the tell-all interview, the leaked love note, the Instagram oops – peels back the glossy veneer to reveal the human truth underneath. Often there's a touch of farce in the reveal. We can't help but chuckle imagining the royal handlers frantically trying to put the genie back in the bottle (*"Maybe no one noticed?"* – spoiler: we noticed). The contrast between the polished myth and the unscripted reality can be downright comical. It's like seeing a majestic swan that suddenly slips on a banana peel. One minute, regality and grace; the next, feathers and squawking. You feel a bit bad for laughing – but you laugh anyway.

Public Fascination vs. Private Reality

Why are we so utterly riveted by the notion that kings and queens might fight over the TV remote or bicker about who forgot to feed the royal corgis? Perhaps because it's the ultimate confirmation that beneath the crowns and ermine robes, *they're human*. They have squabbles and insecurities and silly pet peeves, just like any couple in suburbia. There's a strange comfort in knowing that the Queen of Wherever might roll her eyes at her husband's lame joke, or that the Emperor of Such-and-such sometimes burns his toast and blames the Empress for distracting him. It levels the playing field of humanity. If even *they* – with all their wealth, privilege, and palaces – can be fallible and occasionally ridiculous, then maybe the rest of us are doing okay with our own messy lives.

The public's fascination with royal private life is almost anthropological. We peer at them as if through the looking glass: *How do these rare creatures behave when no one's watching?* Do they argue about whose turn it is to take out the gilded trash? Does the queen snore? (According to one cheeky former footman's memoir, yes, like a chainsaw, allegedly.) We yearn for any sign that their reality is closer to ours than the storybooks suggest. And often, it is. Modern royals have increasingly acknowledged that "Hey, we're not perfect." Princes William and Harry spoke openly about their mental health struggles and family tensions; Queen Letizia of Spain was caught on video having a tense tiff with her mother-in-law – in church, no less – which went viral and sparked national debate. The veneer of perpetual poise is cracking, bit by bit. And interestingly, rather than diminishing their mystique, these humanizing moments can actually increase public affection – up to a point. We like our royals relatable, but not *too* relatable. (If they start arguing on *Jerry Springer*, we'll have gone too far.)

For the royal couples themselves, living under this unblinking spotlight is a delicate tightrope walk. They're expected to symbolize an ideal – the perfect marriage, the model family, a living embodiment of national stability – while actually trying to make a real marriage work. Imagine having millions of strangers perpetually evaluating your relationship based on how often you hold hands at events, or whether you smile at each other during a parade. It's marriage as performance art, 24/7. Any couple would find that tough, let alone with the pressure of upholding dynastic continuity and national morale. One former royal summed it up poignantly (and yes, with a dash of Diana-level honesty):

the public was not to be disappointed, so the show went on, even while there was "a lot of anxiety going on within our four walls." In other words, the palace may be glittering on the outside, while inside the stress and sorrow build up. Royal couples must constantly calibrate: How much of "us" do we show? How much do we hide? Too much authenticity, and they risk undermining the mystique of royalty. Too little, and they seem aloof or fake, and tabloids will simply invent drama to fill the void. It's a no-win scenario that nonetheless has to be navigated daily.

The digital age has only made this balance more challenging. Once upon a time, when the TV cameras stopped, royals could retreat to privacy. Now, the cameras never truly stop rolling. Every smartphone in every bystander's pocket is a potential paparazzo. A king could be having a quiet, off-duty moment at a pub, teasing his wife about her darts skills, and someone will film it and put it on TikTok by dessert. There is no off-the-clock in the age of social media. This reality has forced royals to become more guarded in some ways – and more savvy in others. Some have leaned in, using personal Instagram accounts to share controlled peeks behind the curtain (a casual family selfie here, a home video of the prince changing a diaper there) to satisfy the public's curiosity on *their* own terms. Others have retreated, fiercely defending what shreds of privacy they can (locking down estates, suing paparazzi, etc.). Most do a bit of both, learning the hard way that you can't completely hide, but you can try to steer the narrative.

In the end, the saga of royal public image vs private reality offers a cautionary tale that's surprisingly universal. You don't have to be a king or queen to get it – just think of the last time you posted a smiling family photo on Facebook right after having a huge argument with your spouse or kids. (We've all been there: "Say cheese, or else!") In a sense, many of us are our own little monarchs of social media, curating a life of perpetual smiles and sunny days for public consumption, while the true story might be more complicated. The royals are just doing this on an epic scale, with far higher stakes and skillful press secretaries. Their tightrope walk between personal authenticity and public duty is merely a magnified version of the balance so many people try to strike in the age of Instagram perfection.

So the next time you find yourself chuckling at a headline about, say, *"Royal Couple's Cold War Over Netflix Remote – Who Gets to Choose the Show?"*, remember there's a deeper dynamic at play. The spotlight will always focus on the shiny surface – the *myth* of the perfect royal couple – while the shadows hold the truth that they are as imperfect as anyone. We find reassurance, entertainment, and sometimes schadenfreude in that truth. And perhaps the royals, in turn, find a bit of relief in it too. After all, if the world can accept that they occasionally squabble and stumble, maybe they don't have to pretend *quite* so hard all the time. In an era where authenticity is increasingly valued, even our monarchs might benefit from stepping out of the fairy tale every now and then and saying, *"You know what, we're real people – and that's okay."* Until then, the show goes on: the balcony waves, the curated smiles, the impeccable Christmas cards – and behind them, a quietly brewing question of *how long* any family can keep up the act before the next slip. The spotlight is bright and unblinking, but it's in those shadows that the juiciest, most human lessons of royal life unfold. And if nothing else, those lessons make for one heck of a fun story – one we'll be gossiping about for centuries to come.

Chapter 8

Till Kingdom Come… or Not – Royal Breakups and Divorces

Marriages are often marketed as the ultimate fairy tale – especially when there's a crown involved. But what happens after the "happily ever after," when real life creeps in and those fairy-tale weddings start looking more like reality TV drama (but with tiaras)? In royal circles, splitting up has historically been more complicated than just signing some papers and dividing the record collection. The stakes involve crowns, countries, and centuries of tradition. In this chapter, we'll dish on how kings and queens have navigated the minefield of marital meltdowns through the ages. From the days when "divorce" was a four-letter word that could topple a throne, to modern times when even palace press releases use phrases like "conscious uncoupling" (well, almost), you're about to get an inside look at how royals break up – with a healthy dose of humor, of course. Grab your popcorn (or a scone) and let's peek behind the palace doors.

Breaking with Tradition

Once upon a time, divorce was the ultimate dirty word in royal circles. We're talking a taboo so serious that even whispering it in the throne room might get you banished to a remote tower (or at least given a very stern look by the Lord Chamberlain). For centuries, monarchy and marriage were like a gilded cage: once you were in, you stayed in – *no matter what*. The idea that a king or queen might legally ditch their spouse was unthinkable, downright scandalous. The monarchy's stability was tied to the image of a stable royal family, and a breakup threatened to shake the very foundations of the realm.

How taboo was it? Consider that in 1936 a reigning British king fell head-over-heels in love with a glamorous American divorcée – and it cost him the throne. King Edward VIII's infatuation with Wallis Simpson, a woman who had not one but *two* ex-husbands, triggered a constitutional crisis. As the nominal head of the Church of England, Edward was forbidden to marry a divorced person if the ex-spouses were still living. In Wallis's case, both her former husbands were very much alive and kicking, and the British establishment practically fainted at the idea of her becoming queen. Rather than give up his love, Edward chose to give up his crown. "I have found it impossible to carry the heavy burden of responsibility… without the help and support of the woman I love," he said in his famous abdication speech. In other words: *see ya, throne – love comes first*. It was a romantic gesture for the ages (someone pass the tissue), but it rocked the monarchy. A sitting king walking away for love? Unprecedented! Edward's decision "literally shook the foundations of the British monarchy" and created a worldwide sensation.

For the royals, this was the nightmare scenario. Edward VIII's abdication was a one-time-only show… or so they hoped. After that debacle, the royal family doubled down on its "no divorces, please" policy. The next generation grew up with that cautionary tale ringing in their ears: duty to crown must trump personal happiness. For decades, royal divorces remained rare to nonexistent. In fact, mid-20th-century royals would sooner endure *separate bedrooms* and highly awkward public events than utter the D-word. Even in the 1950s, the taboo held firm – Queen Elizabeth's sister Princess Margaret was pressured to abandon her plan to marry a divorced man rather than spark a constitutional scandal. Such was the strength of the unwritten rule that even being *associated* with divorce could derail a royal romance.

But fast forward a few decades, and reality started to intrude on the fairy tale. By the late 20th century, it turns out blue blood doesn't guarantee wedded bliss. Cracks began to appear in the perfect façade of royal marriages, and the palace's strategy of "never complain, never explain" couldn't hide the tabloid headlines forever. The watershed moment came in the 1990s, when not one, not two, but three of Queen Elizabeth II's four children officially ended their marriages. (Her Majesty grimly dubbed 1992 the *"annus horribilis,"* which is Latin for "year of absolute dumpster fires," loosely speaking.) Suddenly, royal divorce went from unthinkable to, if not commonplace, at least *thinkable*. By the '90s, even the stiff-upper-lip British monarchy had to accept that some fairy tales conclude with separate happy endings. In 1992, Princess Anne divorced, and by 1996 both Prince Charles and Prince Andrew had split from their wives. The Queen – head of the very Church that once forbade these breakups – had to swallow the new normal: marriages sometimes fail, even if you're wearing a crown.

The slow, reluctant acceptance of royal reality even got a seal of approval from the Church of England. In 2002, the Church (perhaps reading the writing on the wall) relaxed its rules to allow remarriage under certain circumstances. This landmark decision paved the way for Prince Charles, the future king himself, to marry the love of his life (and long-time partner) Camilla Parker Bowles in 2005. Think about it: a prince who had been divorced (and whose new wife was a divorcée too) could have a church blessing on his union – something utterly unimaginable back in Edward VIII's day. Indeed, times had changed so much that when Prince Harry, Charles's son, married Meghan Markle (herself a divorcée) in 2018, it was met with the Queen's full consent and zero constitutional drama. One royal writer joked they could almost hear King Edward VIII "spinning in his grave" at how far things had come – the once-taboo scenario of a royal marrying a divorcée was now practically routine.

In short, breaking with tradition has been a rocky road. A process that took centuries (and a lot of personal heartache) transformed royal divorce from an earth-shattering scandal into a shrug-inducing fact of life. Today, tabloids still salivate over royal marital troubles, but the constitutional panic button isn't pressed when a prince or princess calls it quits. The crown has, begrudgingly, learned to coexist with the concept of "happily never after." It's been a long journey – from an era when a king surrendered his empire for love, to an era when even future monarchs can split up without anyone losing their head (literally or figuratively).

For Crown or for Love

Royal history is chock-full of soap-opera-worthy showdowns between the demands of duty and the desires of the heart. If you think your last breakup was dramatic, try doing it with an entire kingdom in the balance. In the eternal cage match between heart and crown, the results have been messy, often scandalous, and endlessly fascinating. Sometimes the heart wins, sometimes the crown wins – but as history shows, there are no clean victories in this fight.

Perhaps the wildest example comes from a king who took "I want a divorce" to nuclear levels. King Henry VIII of England – that larger-than-life monarch with an appetite for power, turkey legs, and wives – literally created a new state religion just to escape his first marriage. Talk about a messy breakup! In the 16th century, Henry found himself in a matrimonial pickle: he was married to Catherine of Aragon, but desperate for a male heir and besotted with Anne Boleyn, one of the liveliest ladies of his court. The Catholic Church forbade him from simply tossing aside Catherine (divorce was a no-no), so Henry's solution was essentially, "Fine, I'll start my *own* church!" And he did. He broke away from the Roman Catholic Church and created the Church of England – all so he could annul his marriage and marry his mistress. This audacious move, known as the English Reformation, changed the course of history. Imagine a CEO today who can't get HR to approve his relationship transfer, so he just builds a whole new company to make it happen. That was Henry's approach to love versus duty. Of course, in true dramatic fashion, Henry's love life didn't exactly stabilize after that. He went on to marry Anne Boleyn (who herself would later lose *her* head – literally – when wifely breakups turned into state-sanctioned *execution*, but that's another level of marital discord altogether). Still, Henry's willingness to upend an entire religious order for the sake of his heart's desire remains unparalleled. It's the ultimate example of a king saying, "My way, or I'll make a highway."

Henry VIII's saga might be extreme, but he wasn't the only royal to pit love against the strictures of convention. Fast-forward a few centuries, and we see more subtle (but still consequential) battles between personal happiness and royal responsibility. We've already met Edward VIII – the king who chose love over crown in 1936 – a modern example of a monarch's heart overruling his duty. His abdication was essentially a giant mic drop: choosing the woman he loved meant relinquishing the empire he was born to rule. It's hard to top that for a "for love" gesture. But not all royals could pay such a steep price for following their hearts. More often, they felt compelled (or were flat-out forced) to put duty first, at great personal cost.

Consider Princess Margaret again. In the 1950s, Margaret was caught in a heart-versus-crown dilemma that captivated the world. She was deeply in love with Group Captain Peter Townsend, a dashing war hero – but alas, he was a divorced man. The establishment (church, parliament, you name it) was firmly against their marriage. Being a dutiful royal, Margaret agonized and ultimately announced in 1955 that she would not marry Townsend after all. In her painfully diplomatic public statement, she said she had decided not to marry "mindful of the Church's teachings" and her duty to the Commonwealth. Translation: *duty wins, love loses*. Many Britons sighed (some even cried) at the thought of what might have been – a real-life royal love story thwarted by protocol. The lesson from that chapter? Choosing crown over heart can break more than just the couple's hearts; it can break the public's too.

On the flip side, sometimes royals did chase their hearts, consequences be damned. One early royal breakup literally changed the map of Europe. When King Louis VII of France annulled his marriage to Queen Eleanor of Aquitaine in 1152, he lost one of the greatest duchies in Europe. Eleanor promptly married England's Henry II, taking the vast Aquitaine lands with her – talk about a divorce settlement! Louis basically handed a huge chunk of his kingdom to his rival through that split. Love 1, duty 0 – at least in the short term. (It's as if a celebrity divorce resulted in half the fanbase literally defecting to a rival – not a perfect analogy, but you get the idea.)

The tug-of-war between love and duty has continued in modern royal houses as well. In the late 20th century, one particularly high-profile royal marriage became a battleground of heart vs. obligation: Prince Charles and Princess Diana. Their 1981 wedding was billed as a storybook union, but behind the scenes it was more complicated. Charles had loved Camilla (now Queen Camilla) for years, but pressures of duty and image led him to marry Diana, an appropriate young aristocrat, to be his future queen and the mother of a future king. The result? A union that unraveled in spectacular fashion, with both parties desperately unhappy and seeking affection elsewhere. In a way, Charles's heart (still pining for Camilla) was at odds with the role he was expected to play with Diana. The heart-vs-crown conflict played out in tabloids and TV interviews, as Diana famously quipped, "there were three of us in this marriage, so it was a bit crowded." Eventually, personal happiness (or at least personal sanity) won out: Charles and Diana separated, then divorced – a scenario that would have been unthinkable for an heir to the throne just a generation earlier. The fallout was messy (understatement of the year) and it proved that even when a royal tries to do the "dutiful" thing, the heart has a way of making itself heard – sometimes at great cost to everyone involved.

From Henry VIII's seismic religious schism to modern princes sneaking off for secret weekends with true loves, the dilemmas of crown versus love have spanned eras and continents. Some royals, like Edward VIII, said "heck with it, love comes first" and paid with their crowns. Others, like Princess Margaret, swallowed heartbreak to uphold duty. And in many cases, the struggle itself led to years of scandal or regret. The overarching lesson? In a cage match between heart and crown, there really are no clean victories. Someone – either the royal, their consort, the monarchy's reputation, or all of the above – will get bruised. Yet, time and again, we see these very human royals wrestling with the choice. It's almost comforting, in a strange way: strip away the ermine and scepters, and even kings and queens find that matters of the heart can make a right royal mess.

Dividing the Royal Spoils

Breaking up is hard to do at the best of times; now imagine doing it when you own half a continent or your family *is* the national symbol of unity. When kings and queens split, it's not just about who gets the dog and the summer cottage – it's a high-stakes game of Monopoly with real castles and countries on the board. Think of it as the world's most complicated divorce court, where crowns, titles, lands, and even public sympathy are all part of the settlement. In this section, we take a somewhat irreverent look at how royal couples have divided the spoils when their happily-ever-after turned into an ever-after party of two separate households.

Historically, some royal "divorce settlements" were downright *medieval* – literally and figuratively. If you were a queen consort getting the boot in, say, the 16th century, you'd be lucky to escape with your head (sorry, Anne Boleyn). But if you did manage to get out alive, what next? Often the queen would be sent off to a quiet exile, far from court, with perhaps a small estate or stipend – essentially the royal equivalent of getting the apartment and a year's supply of alimony. In some cases, she might even be shipped back to her father's territory. (One can imagine the awkward conversation: "Hi Dad, uh, I'm back... marriage didn't work out. By the way, I brought a few soldiers as a severance package.") In *theory*, marriages among royals weren't supposed to fail at all – they were political alliances first, personal relationships second. But when they did fail, it often meant a geopolitical earthquake.

Not all splits rearrange the map of Europe. Sometimes it's about money, titles, and personal perks. Modern royal divorces have their own expensive quirks. When Britain's Prince Charles and Princess Diana went through their very public breakup in the 1990s, the eventual divorce settlement was watched more closely than a World Cup final. Diana reportedly received a lump sum of around £17 million, plus a hefty annual allowance to maintain her lifestyle. She got to keep the title "Princess of Wales," but had to give up the style of "Her Royal Highness" – a detail that might seem trivial to us commoners, but was a *very* big deal in royal circles. (Apparently, keeping those little "HRH" letters after your name is like the royal equivalent of keeping your verified blue checkmark on social media. Losing it meant Diana technically had to curtsey to her ex-husband and even her own sons, who retained their HRH status – *the shade!*). It's said the Queen was fine with Diana staying HRH, but Charles insisted she drop it. Who gets the titles can be as contentious as who gets the house.

And speaking of houses: Diana was allowed to keep living in her sumptuous apartments at Kensington Palace – not too shabby as far as post-divorce pads go. She also kept her jewelry (except a particularly fancy tiara that was a loaner from the Queen) and even retained access to the royal family's private jets. Imagine negotiating in divorce court: "I'll take the Gulfstream every other weekend, thank you very much." For a while, it seemed like Diana got a fairy-tale divorce deal (if such a thing exists). Of course, no amount of money or tiaras could fully compensate for what she had endured in that marriage – but the generous settlement was as close as one gets to a royal *"conscious uncoupling."*

Princess Diana's case was extraordinary, but she wasn't the only one divvying up royal spoils. Sarah Ferguson – aka Fergie – who divorced Prince Andrew in 1996, walked away with a considerably slimmer package (reportedly around £2–3 million). Fergie did, however, keep her Duchess of York title – though, like Diana, she lost the "Her Royal Highness." And then there was the delicate matter of custody. Both Diana and Fergie had young children with their princes. Rather than a nasty courtroom brawl, the palace managed it in a very British way: a polite agreement for joint custody, with the children splitting time between parental households (when they weren't away at boarding school). It was probably the most "normal" aspect of these otherwise oh-so-not-normal divorces.

Of course, the "spoils" aren't just material. In the court of public opinion, people *take sides* in royal splits with fervor. Team Diana vs. Team Charles was definitely a thing in the '90s – and public sympathy overwhelmingly went to the wronged Princess of Wales. Tabloids tallied not only the financial payouts, but the *PR* victories. By the time the dust settled, Diana had won the hearts of the people (if not the crown), while Charles had to slowly rehab his image. This is nothing new – back in 1820, King George IV's attempt to divorce Queen Caroline sparked such public outrage that the plan was dropped. In short, a successful post-divorce life can depend on capturing the hearts of the people, even without a crown.

Dividing royal spoils can also lead to some *dark humor.* Case in point: Henry VIII – the poster boy of messy royal breakups – essentially treated wives like collectible items (sorry, Henry, but it's true). When he divorced Anne of Cleves (Wife #4) after a very short, politically convenient marriage, he gave her a generous parting gift. He cheerfully named her his "beloved sister," handed over some prime real estate (including a palace), and a nice allowance. Anne of Cleves smartly accepted this deal (perhaps recognizing that in the spectrum of Henry's exes, she got the best outcome – divorced, *not* beheaded, and set for life). One could joke that she had one of the best divorce settlements in royal history: she got her own palace and didn't have to deal with Henry's temper anymore. Now *that's* a win-win.

In modern times, the image of two royals actually haggling face-to-face over who gets which palace is a bit far-fetched – these decisions are usually handled discreetly by committees and courtiers. But the absurdity remains. Consider a few of the "assets" that might be on the table in a royal split:

➤ **Titles and Styles:** Will the ex still be a Royal Highness or a Prince/Princess of Something? (Keeping or losing those little "HRH" letters becomes a very big deal – it's like the royal equivalent of keeping your verified blue checkmark.)

➤ **Money and Jewels:** From lump-sum payouts to who gets which tiara, the financial settlement can run into the millions and involve some glittering goodies. (Diana got a generous package and kept most of her bling; Fergie's deal was more modest, but she didn't leave empty-handed.)

➤ **Real Estate:** Palaces, castles, apartments – oh my! Deciding who lives where post-divorce can be tricky. Often the monarch will gift the departing spouse a country estate or a plush apartment to soften the blow. (Diana stayed on at Kensington Palace; centuries earlier, Anne of Cleves got Hever Castle as a parting gift from Henry VIII.)

➤ **Custody (Kids and Corgis):** Not just the princes and princesses, but even the royal pets might effectively need a custody arrangement. (Fergie, for instance, reportedly kept her beloved dogs after her split with Andrew.)

➤ **Friends and Staff:** Courtiers and aristocratic pals may quietly choose sides. A royal divorce can split social circles – some friends will gravitate to one camp or the other, and even longtime royal staff might request a change in assignment depending on their loyalties.

➤ **Reputation and Public Sympathy:** Perhaps the biggest "asset" is less tangible – the court of public opinion. In many breakups, one party wins the PR battle (Princess Diana, for example, emerged from her divorce with global adoration, while Charles had to work to rebuild his image). And this is nothing new – back in 1820, King George IV's attempt to divorce Queen Caroline sparked such public outrage that the plan was dropped. In short, a successful post-divorce life can depend on capturing the hearts of the people, even without a crown.

And finally, there's the matter of the future itself. When a crown is involved, a divorce doesn't just end a marriage; it can alter the line of succession or the trajectory of the monarchy. That's one heck of an estate to divide, and it's why even the most amicable royal splits are handled with intense care.

After the Ever After

So the vows have been broken, the crowns possibly set aside, and the royal divorce papers are signed – now what? Life after a royal divorce can take some surprising turns. Do these ex-royals ride off into the sunset, finally free to eat pizza in pajamas without making headlines? Or do they remain forever orbiting the royal universe, unable to fully escape the gravity of the crown? The answer, unsurprisingly, is a bit of both. In this final section, we examine how kings, queens, princes, and princesses rebuild (or at least rebrand) themselves after a marital meltdown. Spoiler: even after the ever after, these folks prove to be remarkably human – sometimes happier, sometimes not, but always interesting.

For some, the post-divorce plan isn't quiet retirement but a kind of *reinvention*. Take Sarah "Fergie" Ferguson, ex-wife of Prince Andrew. Fergie didn't fade away – she went out and built herself a whole new brand. She wrote memoirs, popped up on TV, became a children's book author, and even a spokesperson for things like Weight Watchers. Sure, not all her post-royal endeavors were smashing successes (a few ill-advised money-making schemes earned her negative headlines), but you have to admire the hustle. At one point, she was even seen on a reality TV show in the U.S., gamely trying to sell British "high tea" to an American audience. The fact that a former daughter-in-law of the Queen was now on daytime television hawking her ventures – that's life after the palace for you. It's an extreme example of how a royal divorcee might carve a new identity. No longer "Her Royal Highness," Fergie became, well, *Sarah*, a working single mom with a famous address book. By her own accounts, she was much happier in many ways after escaping the confines of official royal life.

Others remain *in* the royal orbit, carrying on with duties even after a split. Princess Anne, for instance, divorced her first husband in 1992 but soldiered on with her public service as if nothing had happened, her chin held high. (She even remarried a few years later – proving that sometimes you *can* get a second chance at love without causing a constitutional crisis.) Anne is often cited as the embodiment of "keep calm and carry on" – divorce or not, she opened the next village fête on schedule. Stiff upper lip: 1, Scandal: 0.

Then there are the unique cases of surprisingly cordial post-divorce relationships. Imagine divorcing someone and then ending up living under the same roof years later – *as friends*. Sounds wild, but Prince Andrew and Sarah Ferguson have done exactly that. Despite splitting in the '90s, they have remained so close that they actually still share a home at Royal Lodge in Windsor, decades later. Fergie affectionately calls them "the most extraordinary example of a unified family" – essentially, *the happiest divorced couple in the world.* They co-parented their daughters, Princesses Beatrice and Eugenie, with genuine teamwork, even going on family holidays together after the divorce. When asked about it, Sarah has heaped praise on Andrew, calling him the "finest man" she knows. It's enough to make one wonder why they divorced in the first place (the answer: in the early '90s, their young marriage couldn't withstand the pressures and tabloid scandals of the time). But clearly, as best friends and housemates, they function rather nicely. Seeing them together at events – often beaming side by side at their daughters' weddings – offers an oddly heartwarming epilogue. Not every broken fairy tale stays broken; some evolve into a new kind of family arrangement.

Another study in cordial co-existence: Queen Camilla and her ex-husband, Andrew Parker Bowles. You might think that once Camilla married Prince Charles, her ex would be persona non grata in royal circles. Far from it! Parker Bowles stayed on remarkably good terms – practically an honorary family member. The ultimate sign of post-divorce grace came in 2023, when Camilla was crowned Queen beside King Charles, and there in the front-row of Westminster Abbey sat her ex-husband, Andrew, proudly watching his former wife be crowned. Friends say the two are "joined at the hip" and still have lunch together frequently. They managed to turn a failed marriage into a life-long friendship. It's almost sitcom-worthy: *"My Ex-Husband, the Queen's Best Pal."*

Of course, not every royal divorce ends in cozy camaraderie. Some exes keep their distance (understandably so, in the case of very bitter breakups). The late Princess Diana, after her split from Charles, crafted a new role for herself – one that was adjacent to the royal sphere but also independent. Freed from the confines of palace life, she threw herself into humanitarian causes, championing issues like landmine eradication and HIV/AIDS awareness with a passion that redefined her image. Diana famously said she wanted to be "a queen of people's hearts," and in her brief post-divorce life, she truly was. She and Charles did not remain pals – their interactions were mostly limited to co-parenting their sons and enduring the same ceremonial events from opposite ends of the room. But there was a kind of détente toward the end, an understanding that they both had to move forward. Tragically, Diana's story was cut short in 1997, but her post-divorce chapter showed a woman coming into her own, arguably more influential on the world stage *without* a crown than with one.

One inevitable challenge: running into your ex at royal gatherings. Divorced royals often find themselves at the same weddings, funerals, and yes, even coronations, because they're still family. The protocol is simple: keep calm and carry on. Personal feelings are set aside and a united front is presented for the public. (It helps when the seating chart places exes at opposite ends of the ballroom.)

In the end, the "after" of a royal divorce is often the most humanizing chapter. Once the titles are sorted out and the settlements signed, you're left with individuals trying to find happiness and normalcy – whatever that may look like for them. Some remarry and finally get the love story they yearned for (looking at you, Charles and Camilla, a happy ending decades in the making). Some stay single and relish their freedom from royal expectations. Others remain close friends, proving that family can evolve rather than dissolve. And yes, a few continue to generate the occasional scandal (royals will be royals, after all).

One could say that for all the spectacle of a royal wedding, a royal divorce teaches us more about real life. It shows that even those "living in a castle" can struggle in their relationships, feel trapped by expectations, and make wrenching choices to pursue happiness or uphold duty. It also shows that there's life beyond the palace gates – sometimes a *better* life. The crown may be heavy, but once you put it down, you might just find you can breathe easier. As the dust settles, ex-princes and ex-princesses discover what *we* all do after a breakup: you learn, you grow, and if you're lucky, you even learn to laugh about it someday.

And who knows? Perhaps the greatest legacy of royal breakups is that they've made these lofty figures more relatable. Seeing a king choose love over a kingdom, or a princess strike out on her own after a marital meltdown, reminds everyone that fairy tales can take detours and still find a happy (or at least *happier*) ending. The ever after might not be what the storybooks promised – but for many of these royals, the chapter after "The End" is where they truly come into their own. Life goes on, and often it's *much* better once the crowns are off and the real, human journey begins.

Chapter 9

Modern Thrones – Royal Marriage in the 21st Century

In the 21st century, "happily ever after" for royal couples has gotten a millennial makeover. Palace life today includes Instagram accounts, hybrid work-life balance, and even the occasional royal resignation letter. The old rulebook is being rewritten with a wink and a tweet. In this chapter, we explore how modern kings and queens navigate love and marriage in an era when marrying a commoner is cool, social media is the new court gossip, and royal duty sometimes takes a backseat to personal happiness. It's a witty, eye-opening ride through the throne rooms of today's monarchies – where tradition meets Tinder, and tiaras come with troubleshooting guides.

Commoners and Crown Jewels

Once upon a time, marrying a commoner was the ultimate royal rebellion – the kind of scandal that launched a thousand tabloid headlines (and a few abdications). Back in 1936, Britain's King Edward VIII literally gave up his crown to marry Wallis Simpson, an American divorcée. A generation later, Princess Margaret was forced to renounce the love of her life, Group Captain Peter Townsend, because he was divorced – a very public heartbreak in 1955 that showed how rigid royal marriage rules once were. In those days, princes married princesses (or at least aristocratic ladies with double-barreled names), and "commoners" were strictly for fairy tales or secret affairs.

How times have changed. Fast forward to the last half-century, and nearly every royal heir in Europe has cast aside the old rule of marrying only blue-bloods. In fact, over the past 50 years it's *ceased* to be exceptional – it has *gradually become the norm* – for European royalty to marry commoners. Talk about a plot twist worthy of Netflix! In the past couple of decades especially, all of Europe's young crown princes have dispensed with the traditional matchmaking and wed people from *decidedly* non-royal backgrounds. The convention of princes only marrying princesses has been broken like a runaway train smashing through a centuries-old barrier. The result? A refreshing infusion of new blood and real-world perspectives into some very old royal gene pools.

It's hard to overstate how revolutionary this shift has been. Consider that when Prince William married Catherine "Kate" Middleton in 2011, it was the first time in more than **350 years** that an heir to the British throne had married a woman with no aristocratic lineage. (Kate's mother was a flight attendant and her father a flight dispatcher; the Middletons are successful self-made millionaires, not dukes or duchesses.) A few generations ago, Kate might have been deemed far too *normal* to marry a future king – now she's beloved as the poised Princess of Wales. And if you thought *that* was modern, Prince Harry went even further: in 2018 he married Meghan Markle, an American actress who was not only a commoner but also divorced, biracial, and a self-made celebrity with a social media following. By the time Harry popped the question, the royal rulebook had so many pages torn out that his marriage to Meghan – once unthinkable on multiple counts – was embraced by the monarchy (if not *all* the tabloids).

Europe's other royal houses have similar stories. In Norway, Crown Prince Harald caused a national stir in the 1960s by insisting on marrying Sonja Haraldsen – a commoner from Oslo – and he waited nine long years for his father's permission. Love conquered in the end, and today King Harald V and Queen Sonja are a respected royal couple, credited with modernizing the Norwegian monarchy. Their son, Crown Prince Haakon, upped the ante: he married Mette-Marit Tjessem Høiby, a former waitress and single mother with a bit of a "wild child" past. Mette-Marit even publicly confessed to youthful partying and mistakes (including being present where drugs were used) on live TV before their 2001 wedding. Far from derailing the marriage, her honest apology won Norwegians' sympathy – a sign that the public was ready to accept a relatable future princess, imperfect past and all.

Indeed, the feared wave of public opposition to these unconventional royal romances never really materialized. Instead, crowds have cheered these love matches. Marrying "below their station" has arguably *saved* Europe's monarchies by making them more popular and relatable. One commentator noted that the new crop of future queens – including a self-described party girl (Mette-Marit of Norway), a lawyer from Tasmania (Australia's Mary Donaldson, now Crown Princess of Denmark), an economist from Argentina (Queen Máxima of the Netherlands), a speech therapist (Belgium's Queen Mathilde), and a divorced TV newscaster

(Spain's Queen Letizia) – crashed through old barriers and proved to be intelligent, capable consorts who strengthened the royal families. In other words, these commoners-turned-royals have *yet to put a foot wrong*, and many are "brainier than their royal spouses" to boot.

Marrying outside aristocratic circles has also added some much-needed new DNA to Europe's tightly interwoven royal family tree. (No more worries about Habsburg chins or hemophilia genes – at least not if the Crown can help it!) It's as if the royal gene pool finally opened its windows to let in fresh air. Take Sweden, for example: King Carl XVI Gustaf married Silvia Sommerlath, a German-Brazilian commoner he met when she was an interpreter at the Olympics. Their daughter, Crown Princess Victoria, fell in love with Daniel Westling – her personal fitness trainer. He's now Prince Daniel, having traded his gym tracksuit for a tuxedo. Victoria's brother, Prince Carl Philip, made perhaps the most tabloid-headline-generating match: he married Sofia Hellqvist, a former reality TV star and model. Yes, a one-time contestant from a reality show became a real-life princess – and she's doing a fantastic job at it by all accounts (proving that duchesses can come from any background, even reality TV).

Of course, these commoner fairytales aren't without hiccups. There can be culture shock when a "normal" person joins a royal family. They have to learn protocols that seem archaic (How to curtsy correctly? Which fork to use at a state banquet? How to smile through eight hours of charity receptions without wilting?). Sometimes the snootier elements of high society sneer at the newcomers – recall how the British press initially called Kate Middleton "too middle-class" because her mother once worked as a flight attendant, of all things. And Meghan Markle faced blatant racism and snobbery from some commentators who couldn't handle an outspoken American divorcee in the House of Windsor. But by and large, these commoner spouses have revitalized their monarchies. They connect better with the public (having lived a real life outside palace walls), and they remind the royal in-crowd what the world beyond the throne room is like – a dose of reality that every dynasty needs now and then.

The bottom line? What was once the ultimate royal rebellion – marrying a commoner for love – is now practically expected. Modern kings and queens actively choose partners from very non-royal backgrounds, whether airline pilots or journalists or reality TV personalities. Love matches with "normal" folks have revitalized many monarchies, making royal families more relatable and more resilient in a changing world. As one magazine put it, over just two generations non-royals have been welcomed into nearly all of Europe's royal families – and the sky hasn't fallen. Instead, love begets love, and the people cheer. The Crown gets to survive *and* have a bit of fun. Who would have guessed?

Love in the Time of Social Media

If meddling courtiers and nosy prime ministers once made royal courtships complicated, today's royal lovebirds face an even wilder gauntlet: the 24/7 social media circus. Modern royal couples must court and spark under the unblinking eye of the digital age. Dating in the era of Instagram and instant news means sneakily texting under code names, dodging paparazzi drones on secret getaways, and enduring the Twitter peanut gallery's commentary on your every move. It's love in the time of social media – where every "secret" date can become a trending topic by breakfast.

Imagine trying to have a normal romantic dinner when literally anyone in the restaurant can snap a photo and tweet it to the world. That's the reality for today's princes and princesses. Prince William and Kate Middleton, for example, met in college (St. Andrews University) and managed a relatively low-key courtship for a while. But once the press caught wind that the future king had a girlfriend, poor Kate couldn't walk to class without long-lens photographers hiding in hedges. The two even fled to remote corners of the globe for privacy – William reportedly whisked Kate away to the Seychelles for a secret getaway where paparazzi were *hopefully* out of range. In those early 2000s days, social media was nascent, but the tabloids did their best to fill the void. Fast forward to Prince Harry's generation, and it gets even trickier: Harry and Meghan Markle's love story literally began on Instagram DMs. Yes, you read that right – a royal prince scrolling through Instagram like any other millennial, spotted Meghan's photo on a mutual friend's feed, and hit that follow button! Next thing you know, they were chatting privately and arranging a meetup (with perhaps a secret "finsta" account involved to keep things hush-hush). It's a thoroughly modern meet-cute: *Once upon a time in a direct message…*

In their dating phase, Harry and Meghan took extraordinary measures to dodge the spotlight. They managed a few secret rendezvous – including a now-famous trip to Botswana early in their relationship, where they camped under the stars far from prying eyes. But once the media sniffed out the romance, the frenzy was on. Harry, having seen what happened to his mother Princess Diana, was fiercely protective. When some newspapers and online trolls got nasty about Meghan (involving racist undertones and sexism), Harry broke royal protocol to publicly call them out. In a remarkably blunt statement, he condemned "the outright sexism and racism of social media trolls" harassing his girlfriend. If earlier royals worried about disapproving courtiers, now it's millions of strangers on the internet that can inflict real harm. The Twitter peanut gallery can be far more vicious than any courtier in a wig.

Royal weddings, of course, have always been media spectacles – but in the 21st century, they are global *livestreamed* extravaganzas. When William and Kate married in 2011, an estimated 3 billion people worldwide tuned in to watch the fairy-tale ceremony on TV or online. (That's almost half the planet, clutching their popcorn and fascinators.) Not to be outdone, Prince Harry's 2018 wedding to Meghan was streamed everywhere from YouTube to Twitter, with hashtags like #RoyalWedding blowing up. Nearly 30 million Americans woke up at the crack of dawn to watch Harry and Meghan say "I do" on live TV – and then promptly took to social media to meme every moment from Meghan's dress to the smitten look on Harry's face. In the old days, you had a few official photos and next-day newspaper coverage; now we get real-time GIFs, snarky live-tweets, and Instagram filters of the royal carriage procession. It's participatory theater on a global scale.

This constant connectivity creates new challenges for royal couples. They can't even privately argue without someone speculating on Twitter that it signals doom. Every public gesture is overanalyzed frame-by-frame by body language "experts" on YouTube. Did she roll her eyes at his joke? Twitter will notice. Did he forget to hold her umbrella in the rain? Cue the thinkpieces on gender roles. The public commentary is relentless, and it comes from all corners of the globe in real time. For instance, when unfounded rumors about William's fidelity once swirled on social media, it "caught on like wildfire" despite zero evidence, illustrating how quickly a baseless tweet can create a PR headache. Modern royals must have nerves of steel and the savviness of a PR firm just to survive the daily onslaught of opinions.

On the flip side, social media also lets royal couples write their own narratives in a way previous generations couldn't. Many have official Instagram or Twitter accounts where they share carefully curated peeks into their lives – cute family photos, charity work snapshots, a casual behind-the-scenes moment. This lets them connect directly with the public and bypass some of the tabloids' nonsense. Prince William and Princess Kate, for example, have used social media to present a more personal, relatable image of the monarchy. They post their children's homemade birthday pictures and tweet about mental health initiatives, striking a tone that says "Hey, we're people too (just with very unusual day jobs)." Meghan and Harry took it a step further: before stepping back from royal duties, they amassed millions of Instagram followers on their @SussexRoyal account, using it to make big announcements. In fact, it was on Instagram that they shockingly announced their plan to step back as senior royals in 2020 – a thoroughly modern (and somewhat ironic) way to deliver earth-shaking royal news.

Of course, many royals also maintain *private* social media to actually talk with friends or even to court each other away from prying eyes. In one amusing revelation, royal biographers discovered that Prince Harry ran a secret Instagram account under the name @SpikeyMau5 (a nod to his favorite DJ Deadmau5) during his courtship with Meghan. Meghan followed that private account, and they could flirt in DMs without the press seeing. Imagine the prince sliding into your DMs with a pseudonym – how delightfully clandestine! Other young royals are rumored to have their own low-key accounts on Facebook or Insta, using nicknames to chat with college buddies or even potential dates. It's a far cry from the love letters of yore delivered by footmen; today Cupid's arrow might arrive via WhatsApp encryption.

All this connectivity comes at a cost: *privacy*. Modern royal couples have to fight for every scrap of it. They've gotten creative – from wearing disguises (it's said one European prince used to don a baseball cap and fake mustache to take his girlfriend to the movies incognito) to having friends host gatherings at remote estates to avoid leaks. Some reportedly use encrypted messaging apps and code names in their phones (no "Kate ❤" in Will's contacts – better to use a code word!). Despite these efforts, complete privacy is elusive. The moment a relationship is public, the paparazzi will give chase. But at least the couples can savor the secret phases while they last, crafting their love stories away from the hashtags until duty calls.

In summary, modern royal romance unfolds under a social media microscope. Courting involves as much strategy as a game of chess: covert meetings, digital alias accounts, and media savvy are essential. When they finally tie the knot, it's not just a family affair but a global event dissected tweet by tweet. The pressures are immense – if you thought meddling grand viziers were bad, try millions of online strangers debating your every decision in real time. Yet somehow, today's royal couples are making it work. They leverage the connectivity for good, amplifying charitable causes and showing a human side, even as they tune out the trolls. Love in the time of social media is complicated, yes, but it's also oddly romantic: these couples prove that even with the whole world watching (and commenting), it's possible to build a genuine partnership. You just might need a good VPN and a healthy sense of humor.

The New Rules of Royal Romance

Forget the old fairytale script of meek princesses and stoic princes. In the 21st century, royal marriage comes with a new set of unwritten rules – a version 2.0, if you will. Today's royal spouses are as likely to have careers, causes, and Twitter followers as they are to have tiaras and coat-of-arms stationery. Gender roles that were rigid for centuries are getting a much-needed rewrite: queens consort can be outspoken businesswomen, and princes might be stay-at-home dads or vocal humanitarians. The modern royal marriage is more egalitarian and transparent than ever, though still with a few quirky constraints that linger like ghosts at the banquet (old habits die hard in palaces).

One major shift is that a royal wife is no longer expected to just smile, produce heirs, and cut ribbons at charity events. She can have opinions – even *gasp* a professional background and a voice in public life. Case in point: Queen Letizia of Spain, once a prominent television journalist, hasn't exactly become a silent wallflower since marrying King Felipe VI. She's engaged in issues from education to social causes, bringing savvy media skills from her former career. Queen Máxima of the Netherlands worked in finance and still champions microfinance and women's empowerment on the global stage (she's literally a UN special advocate). These women aren't content to only wave from carriages; they have platforms and aren't afraid to use them. Even Britain's Catherine, Princess of Wales (Kate), though not outspoken politically, has carved out a role focusing on early childhood education and mental health – areas she's clearly passionate about and knowledgeable in from years of study and charity work. Today's princess might have a college degree and a charity initiative rather than a retinue of ladies-in-waiting educating her on court gossip.

Meanwhile, royal husbands have also shed the old "strong, silent, in-charge" stereotype when their wives are the ones in the spotlight. The world got a preview of this dynamic in the last century with Prince Philip, Duke of Edinburgh, who walked two steps behind Queen Elizabeth II for over 60 years. Philip eventually found ways to lead in his consort role (he ran charities, managed the royal estates, and was the family's unofficial CEO), but it wasn't easy for a 1950s man to accept playing second fiddle. In the 21st century, however, men marrying powerful women are more comfortable in supportive roles. Sweden offers a wonderful example: when Crown Princess Victoria becomes queen one day, her husband Prince Daniel will be *Prince Consort* with no constitutional power — and he's just fine with that. A former personal trainer and self-made businessman, Daniel has already shown that his primary job is being Victoria's rock and an involved dad to their two children. He even openly took parental leave when their kids were born, a concept that would have boggled Prince Philip's mind back in the day. It's increasingly common to see princes pushing strollers and changing diapers (Prince William famously earned a "badge of honor" by doing the first diaper change for baby George himself). Royal fathers today talk about the school run and bedtime routines — William and Kate have spoken about trying to give their kids a "normal" childhood, with William even dropping off Prince George at school in the mornings like any other dad (albeit one with police escorts discreetly in tow).

This more egalitarian approach is evident in how William and Kate are shaping their family life. They openly prioritize mental health, family wellness and work-life balance, bringing a "fresh honesty" to royal life that previous generations never did. The couple has made it a point to be hands-on parents — they've been seen playing with their kids in the park and doing school pickups, activities that Queen Elizabeth II certainly never did (nannies handled all that in her era). By leading in this way, William and Kate reflect *millennial values* inside the monarchy. They use technology and social media to connect with people, champion causes like climate change and mental health, and make it clear that family comes first even as they fulfill royal duties. This is a sea change from the "duty above all, never explain, never complain" mantra of Elizabeth's time. Modern royals *do* explain – they share their struggles, whether it's Kate talking about the challenges of motherhood or William discussing grief and mental health. They even, on occasion, complain (Harry certainly has, quite publicly, about the pressures his family faced). It's a more transparent approach to royal marriage and family, showing that royals are human and that a strong marriage is a partnership of equals as much as possible.

Another new rule of royal romance: it's okay to break some old rules, so long as you uphold the important traditions. For example, it used to be unheard of for a royal couple to show any PDA (public display of affection) on official outings – but now we occasionally see a warm hug or hand-hold. Harry and Meghan were often spotted holding hands at events, a small but significant departure from the stiff formality of previous royal pairs. Even the more reserved William and Kate have been caught on camera exchanging a loving glance or a quick touch on the back during engagements. These are tiny humanizing moments that would have made Queen Victoria gasp, yet today they make royals seem more relatable. Royal spouses also now attend events that once excluded them: in earlier times, the wives of kings didn't typically attend cabinet swearing-ins or military briefings; now, queens consort like Letizia or Máxima might sit in on certain official meetings related to their interests. Princes like Daniel of Sweden or Prince Albert of Monaco (who is consort to his reigning wife, Princess Charlene) support their wives' agendas and sometimes have causes of their own. The old male pride that might have been wounded by a wife with a higher status is (slowly) fading. As one Danish prince quipped when asked if he felt overshadowed by his queen-in-waiting wife, "Not at all – I shine in her light." That might be the sweetest job description for a modern prince consort.

However, lest we think monarchy has become a total free-for-all, *some* old-school expectations still cling on – those "ghosts at the banquet" of tradition. For instance, despite modernization, royalty is still royalty. A future queen like Kate Middleton is expected to *eventually* produce an "heir and a spare" (which she dutifully did – three kids in her case), and to do so without grumbling about the pressure. The expectation to continue the bloodline is one tradition that hasn't relaxed much; it's just discussed less openly now. Another lingering rule: deference to the monarch. Even a very modern royal wife must technically curtsy to her husband's grandmother (the Queen) or now to her father-in-law (the King), and to certain other princesses depending on who's in the room. These Byzantine protocols of who bows to whom persist, to the bewilderment of commoner spouses trying to learn the hierarchy. Dress codes also remain somewhat archaic – women in the British royal family still wear hats at formal day events and tiaras at state dinners, and there's an *unwritten* expectation to dress modestly and never outshine the monarch. (Meghan learned this the hard way when even a slight deviation like not wearing nude pantyhose became tabloid fodder – apparently bare legs were a no-no in the Queen's presence. Who knew?)

Then there's the injunction against expressing political opinions. Modern royals can have opinions, but they must be *carefully* packaged as charitable endeavors or personal initiatives. For example, Prince Harry and Meghan felt constrained by this when Meghan, who had been an outspoken advocate on women's issues as a private citizen, had to dial back her public commentary after marriage. Prince Charles (now King Charles III) pushed the envelope for years by speaking about the environment and architecture – causes he framed as non-partisan, though some critics grumbled even that was too political. The younger generation is continuing this balancing act: they speak on social issues like mental health or climate change (widely seen as acceptable areas), but they avoid party politics or anything too controversial. So while a modern royal couple might share their struggles with postpartum depression or campaign for mental health awareness – displays of honesty that were unheard of decades ago – they will still refrain from, say, endorsing a candidate or marching in a protest. The crown remains studiously neutral, and that expectation still looms over even the most progressive royal marriages.

We also see tradition pop up in the most personal decisions. Naming of royal children, for instance, remains a careful nod to history; you won't see a Princess Madison or Prince Jayden anytime soon – it's still George, Charlotte, Louis (in Britain) or traditional names like Estelle and Oscar (in Sweden's royal family). And when it comes to weddings, many of the age-old customs are kept: huge cathedral ceremony, ancient title grants, tons of pomp. Modern royals embrace the romance of those traditions even as they update other aspects. They might invite a mix of A-list celebrities *and* charity workers to their wedding (as Harry and Meghan did) – blending the old aristocratic guest list with a new, inclusive twist. They'll kiss on the palace balcony for the crowds (a relatively new tradition since Charles and Diana started it in 1981, but now a must), then perhaps head to an evening reception with a trendy DJ and organic canapés instead of crumbling fruitcake alone.

All in all, a royal marriage 2.0 operates with far more equality and openness than ever before. Today's royal couples often strive to present themselves as a team. They share duties more evenly, and sometimes even swap traditional roles. It's not unusual now to see a queen consort give a speech or have a solo project that gets top billing, while her king quietly supports in the background – something almost unheard of a century ago. Princes who aren't the heir (the "spares") often go out and have careers or start their own ventures, which brings a dose of real-world experience back into the family. For example, Princess Anne's children, Zara and Peter, have no royal titles and have built private careers (Zara is an Olympic equestrian). This would have been unthinkable for Queen Victoria's children, for example, but it's normal now.

Yet, even as things have come far, the monarchy can still feel like a quirky anachronism. Royals are trying to be relatable – driving their kids to school, talking about mental health – while still living in palaces and wearing crowns at state openings of parliament. The cognitive dissonance can be amusing. It's a bit like trying to be a relatable social media influencer while also adhering to a 1,000-year-old dress code – a strange juggling act that today's royal couples perform daily. They have to live on Instagram and in ancient ivory tower institutions at the same time.

The progress is real and worth celebrating: *marriages are stronger and royals happier when they marry for love and can be themselves.* The new rules of royal romance have made the Windsors, Bourbons, Glücksburgs and more much more in tune with the modern world. But as any royal will tell you, some traditions die hard. Those ghosts at the banquet – duty, protocol, decorum – still hover, occasionally rattling their chains to remind everyone that being royal is *never* going to be exactly like being normal. The trick for 21st-century royal couples is figuring out how to honor the past without being trapped by it. So far, they're managing – with a healthy dose of humor, mutual support, and the knowledge that sometimes you just have to nod to tradition, then quietly do your own thing anyway.

Stepping Away from the Palace

Perhaps the most startling development in modern royal life is this: a royal couple can choose to step back from official duties for the sake of their marriage and mental health – and *survive* to tell the tale. In fact, not only survive, but thrive in a new life. Once upon a time, "divorcing" the Crown was virtually unthinkable (the lone example, Edward VIII in 1936, lived out his days in exile for choosing love over duty). But today, we've entered an era of royals effectively saying, "You know what? We'd like a partial royal *quit*, please," and the monarchy (after some heartburn) accommodating it. It's a development that would have given the palace gray hairs a few generations ago. Now it's becoming almost – dare we say

– normal for younger royals to prioritize personal well-being over relentless duty. Love may finally be conquering the last bastion of tradition: the notion that royalty is a lifelong cage you can't escape from.

The poster couple for this trend is, of course, Prince Harry and Meghan Markle. In early 2020, they dropped a bombshell announcement (on Instagram, no less) that they intended to "step back as 'senior' members of the Royal Family" and work toward becoming financially independent. In plain terms, they quit the royal day jobs and moved abroad to seek a happier life. It was unprecedented in modern British history – a king's grandson saying "no thanks" to the royal grind – and it sent shockwaves through the monarchy. Yet it happened. After a brief family summit (dubbed the "Sandringham Summit"), the Queen gave her reluctant blessing, saying she supported Harry and Meghan's desire for a more independent life even though she "would have preferred them to remain full-time working members" of the royal family. There would be a transition period, she noted, and by March 2020 the Duke and Duchess of Sussex were officially out: they gave up their royal patronages, stopped using their HRH titles, and headed to North America. Essentially, they resigned from The Firm (as the British royals call the institution) – something once thought about as likely as the Pope quitting the Vatican.

The reason behind this dramatic move? In a word, *sanity*. The couple had faced a torrent of negative media attention, internal family tensions, and felt their personal happiness was at stake. Harry later likened their situation to being trapped and said he didn't want history repeating itself (a reference to his mother Diana's tragic experience). Meghan spoke openly about struggling with her mental health under the pressure and even having suicidal thoughts during her pregnancy, which horrified Harry and spurred him to protect his wife and child at all costs. For these two, stepping away from palace life was a matter of emotional survival. And indeed, once they left, a friend noted "it's got to feel like an immense relief to get out…and go down their own path". They ended up in California, carving out a new semi-private life – signing Netflix deals, launching charitable initiatives, raising their kids Archie and Lili largely out of the spotlight. In a twist of fate, their "happily ever after" is unfolding outside palace walls, not in them.

Harry and Meghan's quasi-"abdication" was a wake-up call: it showed that the golden royal cage had an escape hatch after all. The sky did not fall; the monarchy is continuing (albeit with some bruised feelings and a lot of media drama). In fact, the Queen's remarkably understanding statement set a precedent that you *can* be a beloved member of the family even if you're not actively doing royal duties. This was a revolution in thinking – earlier monarchs likely would have slammed the door shut (remember, when Edward VIII left, he and Wallis were essentially ostracized). Now, the message is: *we prefer you stay, but if you must go, you're still family*. It's almost "have your cake and eat it too" – Harry and Meghan kept their Duke and Duchess titles and a place in the family, even as they stopped carrying out royal work. Sure, there were consequences (no more public funding, loss of honorary military appointments, etc.), but compared to exile, it's a pretty sweet deal. They still get to be called "Your Royal Highness" (technically) without the burden of endless public engagements.

This development begs the question: what does it mean for the future of monarchy when *happily ever after* might occur outside the palace? One thing it means is that the younger generation takes the concept of mental health and personal happiness very seriously – even more seriously than fealty to a role they were born into. Prince William and Princess Kate, while very much dedicated to the Crown, have also made clear that their family's well-being comes first. They likely won't step away (barring something unforeseen) because William is destined to be king, but they have adjusted the role to be more human. For royals further down the line of succession, however, Harry and Meghan's path might look appealing: you can step out of the spotlight, move to Malibu (or wherever), and still be *okay*. Essentially, they demonstrated an escape route for the "spares" especially, those who aren't going to sit on the throne and might feel stifled as mere support acts. It wouldn't be surprising if in the coming decades more minor royals say "I'm out." In fact, some already have in their own ways – King Carl XVI Gustaf of Sweden slimmed down his monarchy by removing many of his grandchildren (those not in direct line) from the official royal roster, freeing them to have normal lives. Princess Märtha Louise of Norway (King Harald's daughter) stepped back from royal duties to pursue her own career as a holistic healer and to live partly in the US with her fiancé. And in Japan, we've seen Emperor Naruhito's niece, Princess Mako, *completely* leave the Imperial Family in 2021 to marry her college sweetheart – no half-measures there, she gave up her title and status entirely to be with the man she loves.

Princess Mako's case in Japan is illuminating because it parallels Harry and Meghan's in some ways, though in an even stricter system. Japanese law requires princesses to lose their royal status if they marry a commoner, so Mako knew she was effectively "abdicating" her princess life for love. She did it anyway, marrying Kei Komuro, a regular guy (albeit with a law degree) – and the two moved to New York City to start fresh. The pressures they faced in Japan were intense: years of frenzied media scrutiny and public controversy over a minor financial dispute involving Kei's mother took such a toll that Mako was diagnosed with post-traumatic stress disorder (PTSD) before the wedding. Yes, the negative media coverage literally gave a princess PTSD – talk about a clear sign that something in the system was broken. Mako said marrying Kei was a "necessary choice" for their well-being, despite knowing many in the public disapproved. In a poignant press conference, she expressed hope for a society "where we can all live and support each other's feelings". It was essentially a plea for empathy over protocol. Now Mako and Kei are living a quiet life in the US, and she's the first Japanese royal woman in modern memory to essentially choose love and mental health over palace duty. Her story drew comparisons even in Japanese media to Harry and Meghan's exit, suggesting a broader trend: across cultures, younger royals are asserting the right to *normalcy* and happiness, even if it means breaking with tradition.

Not every royal step-back is quite so dramatic, but the concept of a part-time or self-selected royal role is certainly more accepted now. Some European monarchies have built in a kind of gentle off-ramp: in the Netherlands and Belgium, monarchs have felt free to abdicate (retire) in favor of the next generation once they felt they'd done their part. That's a different scenario (mostly age-related), but it contributes to the idea that serving as monarch or royal is a role, not a divinely ordained identity you must cling to until death. If a monarch can retire for the good of the country (as Queen Beatrix of the Netherlands did in 2013, passing the throne to her son), then surely a royal who isn't even the sovereign can retire for the good of their own family.

This "have your cake and eat it too" approach – where royals try to have a foot in both worlds – does come with controversy. Critics argue, for example, that Harry and Meghan traded on their royal titles while not doing the work, essentially monetizing their royalty. The Sussexes counter that they simply wanted to earn their own income and have a more peaceful life, and that the only ones making money off royalty were the tabloid press. Regardless of where one stands, the fact remains they *did* carve out a new model. They were financially cut off from the royal purse and had to fund themselves, but they kept their identities as Duke and Duchess and the global platform that comes with that. In earlier eras, leaving royalty meant fading into obscurity; now it can mean a lucrative Spotify podcast deal and appearances on Oprah. This is new terrain. Monarchy purists find it troubling, but many younger people find it perfectly reasonable – why shouldn't a couple protect their mental health and still call grandma (who happens to be the Queen) on the weekend? As Queen Elizabeth II herself said in her unusually personal statement, "my family and I are entirely supportive of Harry and Meghan's desire to create a new life as a young family". It was a remarkable acknowledgment that royal or not, they are first and foremost a young family in need of happiness.

What does all this portend for the future? We might see a kind of "royal flexitime" become a thing – where certain royals have the option to step in and out of official duty over their lifetimes. Already, there are "non-working royals" in most families (think of Queen Elizabeth's other grandchildren like Princess Beatrice and Princess Eugenie, who have regular jobs and only occasional royal duties). The boundary between being a private citizen and a royal is blurring. Monarchies may streamline to only the core heirs doing full-time duty, while others quietly bow out. This could actually help keep monarchies afloat – fewer people on the public payroll, less tabloid fodder from disillusioned junior royals, and happier individuals who aren't forced into a mold that doesn't fit. On the other hand, if too many opt out, one wonders, who's left to actually ribbon-cut and shake hands for the firm? There is an existential balance to maintain.

One thing is clear: the mystique of "royalty as cage" is fading. The last bastion of tradition – the idea that royal duty always trumps personal desire – has been challenged head-on by love and personal choice. It's poetic, really: love triumphing in the end, even in the context of ancient institutions. Once, a king gave up everything for love and it rocked the monarchy. Now, a king's grandson can give up a little for love (not the throne, but the trappings) and the monarchy adapts. As the Queen herself said in her 90s, "evolution, not revolution" is the key to monarchy's survival. The evolution here is allowing royals to be human beings who can say *enough* when duty overwhelms happiness.

In a romantic comedy version of this scenario, you'd have the prince and princess making a grand escape from the palace to find their bliss in the wild world, and eventually everyone learns to be okay with it. Reality isn't quite so neat – family rifts and public debates continue – but fundamentally Harry and Meghan are *okay*, and so are the royals they left behind. Other couples see that it's possible. Monarchy didn't crumble; it bent and adjusted. This opens up imaginative possibilities: perhaps a future queen and her husband might decide to take a sabbatical year to raise their infant in peace, or a royal couple might choose to live abroad for a time if their careers demand it, without causing a national crisis.

We end with a provocative thought: maybe *happily ever after* for royals doesn't always mean prince and princess on a throne. Maybe it can mean prince and princess on a quiet farm somewhere, or running a non-profit in Africa, or, heck, hosting a Netflix documentary series about causes they care about. The institution of royalty is slowly being reshaped to accommodate personal fulfillment. It turns out that when royal couples put their marriage and mental well-being first, the monarchy doesn't die – it might actually thrive because it shows adaptability. The ultimate goal, after all, is for these very public marriages to succeed and for the individuals in them to remain sane and relatable. If that occasionally means stepping away from the palace, so be it. In the grand battle of love vs. duty, love is gaining ground. And for royal couples, that's a fun fact indeed – one that might ensure their *real* happily ever after, cameras or no cameras.

Chapter 10
The Royal We – Lessons (and Laughs) from Regal Unions

Royal marriage – just the phrase conjures images of gilded carriages, glittering tiaras, and fairy-tale romance. But after delving into the love lives of kings and queens, one thing is clear: uneasy lies the marriage bed that's draped in royal satin. When the cameras stop rolling and the crowns come off, a palace can be less "happily ever after" and more a high-drama household with a very fancy mailing address. As we've seen through these tales, marrying into royalty is no fairy-tale picnic. The opulence comes packaged with operatic drama, and "it's good to be king" often doesn't apply to one's home life.

Uneasy Lies the Marriage Bed

If there's one big takeaway from all these regal romances, it's that tying the knot with a monarch is a mixed blessing at best. Sure, you get palaces, jewels, and an army of servants to do the washing up. But you also inherit centuries of baggage and a spotlight so bright it could give anyone a royal migraine. Consider the cautionary tales: Princess Diana went into her marriage expecting a storybook ending, only to find her Prince Charming already had a well-established *affection* for someone else. (She famously quipped that her marriage was "a bit crowded" – apparently three's a crowd even when one of you is wearing a coronet.)

The world watched Diana's lavish wedding and envied her gigantic sapphire engagement ring, but behind closed doors the relationship devolved into a soap opera no amount of tiaras could fix. The lesson? Even a twenty-foot train and cathedral vows can't guarantee marital bliss when you've got crown-sized pressures bearing down on the relationship.

And how about King Henry VIII – the poster child for why marrying royalty can be hazardous to your health (literally, in his spouses' case)? When the marital going got tough, Henry got chopping. This was a man who took "irreconcilable differences" to a whole new level – if a wife displeased him, he didn't call a divorce lawyer, he called the executioner. Henry wasn't big on compromise or counseling; he preferred an axe. The poor women who married him had to worry not just about *meeting the parents* but *keeping their heads*. It's an extreme example, sure, but it drives home the point: being queen consort in the 16th century was no fairy tale. (Anne Boleyn might prefer the word "nightmare.") The very things that make royal life enviable – the power, the wealth, the legions of advisors – can act like gasoline on the fire of a marriage. Minor squabbles that any couple might have ("You spent *how much* on new tapestries?") can become international incidents or matters of state. Privacy is nonexistent; every spat could fuel a hundred court whispers or, nowadays, tabloid headlines.

Living in a castle with a crown on your head is bound to magnify every marital issue. Did the king leave his socks on the floor? That's not just a domestic quibble – it might be seen as a breach of protocol. Did the queen roll her eyes at the king's idea? Cue the advisors fretting about "discord in the realm." It sounds absurd, but history gives us plenty of examples of domestic tiffs that escalated thanks to royal ego and public scrutiny. All this regal drama makes one appreciate the simple bliss of an ordinary life with an ordinary love. When your evening entertainment is Netflix on the couch instead of a state dinner with bickering courtiers, you've already eliminated about ninety percent of the stress these royal couples faced. No gold thrones, no tiaras, no nosy palace aides – just two people and maybe an argument over who forgot to buy milk. Sounds positively peaceful by comparison! An ordinary spouse may occasionally banish you to the living room sofa after a fight; a royal spouse might literally banish you to another castle for a "cooling off" period. (Having a spare castle or two can come in handy for that, as many a medieval king knew.) So the next time we commoners daydream about trading places with a royal couple, we should remember that along with those chauffeured Bentleys comes the chance of your marital squabbles ending up in history books or on the front page. Suddenly, that quiet, ordinary love – with all its modest annoyances – seems like a blessing.

Power vs. Partnership

Royal couples provide an exaggerated mirror of the eternal struggle in marriages everywhere: balancing two individuals' needs, ambitions, and identities. When one half of the couple literally wears a crown, that balance can get skewed faster than you can say "Your Majesty." Being married to a king or queen isn't just a relationship; it's a day job (with terrible hours and absolutely no casual Fridays). In a healthy marriage, both partners should feel equal – but what if one partner's face is on the coins and the other is technically their subject? Awkward.

History books overflow with royal pairs who never quite figured out the partnership part. Often, the monarch's word was law and the spouse was expected to smile, produce heirs, and not make a fuss. That kind of one-sided power dynamic would challenge even the most saintly of partners. Look at Catherine the Great and her hapless husband Peter III: their arranged royal marriage was so imbalanced that she literally overthrew him. Peter was more interested in playing with toy soldiers than in his real-life wife; Catherine, armed with ambition and savvy, decided to seize power for herself. Before long, Peter was ousted and "conveniently" died under mysterious circumstances. Lesson: if one spouse treats the other like a pawn, don't be surprised when the queen takes the king.

These stories illustrate that even in palaces – perhaps *especially* in palaces – respect and compromise aren't just plebeian virtues; they're vital for survival. When monarchs forget that, they do so at their peril (sometimes literally losing heads, crowns, or marriages). If there's a silver lining in studying these royal matrimonies, it's seeing that the happiest regal unions – however rare – all boil down to partnership. A king and queen who treat each other as allies rather than adversaries stand a much better chance of keeping their heads (again, looking at you, Henry) and their hearts intact.

Consider the British royals: Queen Elizabeth II and Prince Philip had to navigate a delicate dance of power and partnership. She was the reigning monarch; he was a confident naval officer used to command. When she became Queen, Philip had to literally walk two steps behind his wife and even give up his naval career – a bitter pill for any man of ambition. It could have spelled doom at home, but to their credit they figured it out. Over decades together, the Queen and Philip struck a balance: he carved out a role as her supporter-in-chief (and court jester, on occasion), and she valued his candid, irreverent advice. Those stuffy courtiers who once whispered that Philip was "too undignified" for her were proven wrong – it turns out a strong partnership sometimes needs a strong sense of humor. In fact, Philip's infamous gaffes and one-liners (the kind of off-the-cuff remarks that would get lesser mortals sent to the couch) were often met by Elizabeth with an eye-roll and a laugh. She understood what even ordinary couples know: respect, communication, and the ability to chuckle at life's absurdities are key.

On the flip side, we've seen what happens when power utterly outweighs partnership. Many a king treated his queen as just another subject – or worse, a decorative womb with a crown attached. Without an even partnership, things can go south quickly. The tragic fates of Henry VIII's wives, the downfall of hapless Peter III, the turmoil of so many royal unions – they all underscore that even monarchs ignore basic relationship truths at their peril. Respect and compromise aren't just virtues for peasants; even kings and queens break the rules of marriage at great risk.

They're Just Like Us (No, Really!)

Amid all this talk of crowns, castles, and intrigue, it's easy to forget a simple fact: underneath the regalia, royals are human beings. Shocking, I know! But seriously – one reason we're so fascinated by royal couples is that their lives, though extreme, illuminate universal truths about marriage. In their extravagant ups and downs, we recognize our own experiences (just with more zeros on the budget and more diamonds in the jewelry box). They fight about money, they have in-law drama, they deal with parenting headaches and personal loss. Strip away the scepters and ermine robes, and you find that kings and queens argue over both trivial things and profound ones, just like any couple anywhere.

Take something as mundane as squabbles over spending. Every couple disagrees about money at some point – maybe one loves shopping while the other insists on saving. Well, imagine that problem when you're literally in charge of a national treasury. Marie Antoinette wasn't exactly clipping coupons; she took a lot of heat for her extravagant spending on gowns, gambling, and parties. Meanwhile, her husband Louis XVI was off tinkering in his locksmith workshop, seemingly oblivious to the mounting bills (and the mounting public anger). For all their squabbles over finances – her expensive tastes, his oblivious tinkering – the stakes were absurdly high. A disagreement over the budget in their case wasn't just about belt-tightening; it helped fan the flames of revolution. (Talk about an extreme outcome for a marital spat.)

And then we have those pesky in-laws. Regular folks might dread awkward holidays with their spouse's family, but imagine your mother-in-law is an Empress who's not shy about giving orders. Marie Antoinette's formidable mom, Empress Maria Theresa, sent her daughter scolding letters about everything – even the urgency of producing an heir. More recently, Britain's "Firm" gave a rather chilly reception to new royal additions. (It's no wonder Prince Harry and Meghan Markle hopped an ocean away to get some breathing room.) The scale is different, but the in-law dramas – overbearing elders, family expectations, meddling advice – are universal.

How about the daily squabbles and annoyances? Those little "Honey, can you *please* not leave your boots in the hallway?" moments. You bet royalty have those too (well, perhaps not the bill-paying, since someone does that for them – nice perk – but other petty arguments). Some royal couples have been infamous for their shouting matches. Princess Margaret (Queen Elizabeth II's sister) and her husband Antony Armstrong-Jones were famously volatile – their screaming matches could be heard throughout the palace. It got so bad that at one point Tony literally climbed out of a window to escape an argument – now *that's* a relatable level of drama (albeit most of us don't have a palace terrace for our grand exits). Even the most buttoned-up royals aren't immune to door-slamming moments. It humanizes them: the idea that somewhere in Buckingham Palace, a prince might be muttering, "Yes, dear, I'll put the toilet seat down," is oddly comforting.

Even the profound sorrows that ordinary families face – illness, loss, heartbreak – visit royal households. The difference is, they have to grieve or struggle with the world watching and commenting. Still, their experiences resonate with us. When Queen Elizabeth II lost her beloved partner Prince Philip after 73 years of marriage, the image of her sitting alone at his funeral was heartbreaking and instantly understood by anyone who has lost a spouse. In that moment she wasn't a Queen – she was a widow mourning her husband, a human being feeling loneliness. If a literal king can slip up and have to grovel for forgiveness, there's hope for the average Joe who left the lid off the toothpaste. And if a queen can publicly forgive her consort for a very embarrassing blunder, surely we can forgive our partners for forgetting an anniversary. Recognizing the humanity in these lofty figures is oddly reassuring: if a marriage that carries the weight of a kingdom can find moments of forgiveness and humor, then maybe our humble unions can too.

Happily Ever After-ish

In the end, the story of royal marriages is not one of pure cynicism or of saccharine fantasy, but something in between. It's a tale of people under ridiculous pressure trying to make love work – sometimes succeeding, often failing, always providing a lesson (or at least a juicy anecdote). "Happily ever after" might be a myth, but "ever after-ish" has a nice ring to it – it implies the story continues, not always smoothly, but with some hope and plenty of humor. As we've learned, when the cameras stop rolling, real life begins for everyone, even those on thrones. And that real life – messy, complicated, poignant, and often funny – is far more interesting than any perfectly scripted fairy tale.

It doesn't hurt that these stories are wildly entertaining. You really can't make this stuff up: a king who abdicates his throne for love, a queen who literally has her spouse arrested – it's like history's ultimate soap opera. And how do we deal with the sheer absurdity of it all? With humor, of course. If we can't chuckle at the image of a mighty king donning an apron to wash dishes as a peace offering to his queen, then what's the point of studying history? That delightful image reminds us that when all the pomp and ceremony are stripped away, at the end of the day it's just a husband and wife in their palace kitchen, trying to keep the peace.

"Happily ever after" might be a myth, but real life ever after – with all its imperfections – is far more compelling. Through the royal highs and lows, we've seen the cost of duty, the need for authenticity, and the remarkable resilience of love. We've also gotten a much-needed laugh at the spectacle of kings and queens being, well, incredibly human. And if we can laugh and learn at the same time, that's a story better than any fairy tale – one where love endures *and* the audience gets a great punchline.

Epilogue

And so we close the golden-hinged doors on centuries of royal matrimonial mayhem, having witnessed everything from Henry VIII's habit of treating wives like disposable dinner plates to modern monarchs navigating prenups thicker than constitutional law. The crown jewels may sparkle, but the real gems have been the deliciously dysfunctional dynamics we've uncovered behind palace walls.

Through tapestries of scandal, we've seen that royalty doesn't immunize against the universal ailments of marriage: snoring spouses, mother-in-law interference, and arguments over who forgot to take out the royal trash. These blue-blooded unions prove that even with unlimited staff, separate wings, and enough tiaras to stock a Broadway costume department, couples still find creative ways to drive each other absolutely mad.

The divorce lawyers may have gotten richer, the tabloids certainly have, and palace staff have developed supernatural hearing loss, but here's the remarkable truth: somehow, against astronomical odds and centuries of evidence suggesting otherwise, people keep falling in love and saying "I do" – even with crowns involved.

Perhaps that stubborn persistence of hope, that willingness to believe this time will be different, that love might actually conquer all (including constitutional crises), represents the most endearing human trait of all.

After all, if royalty can keep trying despite their spectacularly public failures, maybe there's hope for the rest of us commoners yet.

Long live love – and longer live the entertainment value of royal romance.